African Politics: A Very Short Introduction

VERY SHORT INTRODUCTIONS are for anyone wanting a stimulating and accessible way into a new subject. They are written by experts, and have been translated into more than 45 different languages.

The series began in 1995, and now covers a wide variety of topics in every discipline. The VSI library currently contains over 550 volumes—a Very Short Introduction to everything from Psychology and Philosophy of Science to American History and Relativity—and continues to grow in every subject area.

Very Short Introductions available now:

ABOLITIONISM Richard S. Newman
ACCOUNTING Christopher Nobes
ADOLESCENCE Peter K. Smith
ADVERTISING Winston Fletcher
AFRICAN AMERICAN RELIGION
    Eddie S. Glaude Jr
AFRICAN HISTORY John Parker and
    Richard Rathbone
AFRICAN POLITICS Ian Taylor
AFRICAN RELIGIONS
    Jacob K. Olupona
AGEING Nancy A. Pachana
AGNOSTICISM Robin Le Poidevin
AGRICULTURE Paul Brassley and
    Richard Soffe
ALEXANDER THE GREAT
    Hugh Bowden
ALGEBRA Peter M. Higgins
AMERICAN CULTURAL HISTORY
    Eric Avila
AMERICAN HISTORY Paul S. Boyer
AMERICAN IMMIGRATION
    David A. Gerber
AMERICAN LEGAL HISTORY
    G. Edward White
AMERICAN POLITICAL HISTORY
    Donald Critchlow
AMERICAN POLITICAL PARTIES
    AND ELECTIONS L. Sandy Maisel
AMERICAN POLITICS
    Richard M. Valelly
THE AMERICAN PRESIDENCY
    Charles O. Jones
THE AMERICAN REVOLUTION
    Robert J. Allison

AMERICAN SLAVERY
    Heather Andrea Williams
THE AMERICAN WEST Stephen Aron
AMERICAN WOMEN'S HISTORY
    Susan Ware
ANAESTHESIA Aidan O'Donnell
ANALYTIC PHILOSOPHY
    Michael Beaney
ANARCHISM Colin Ward
ANCIENT ASSYRIA Karen Radner
ANCIENT EGYPT Ian Shaw
ANCIENT EGYPTIAN ART AND
    ARCHITECTURE Christina Riggs
ANCIENT GREECE Paul Cartledge
THE ANCIENT NEAR EAST
    Amanda H. Podany
ANCIENT PHILOSOPHY Julia Annas
ANCIENT WARFARE
    Harry Sidebottom
ANGELS David Albert Jones
ANGLICANISM Mark Chapman
THE ANGLO-SAXON AGE John Blair
ANIMAL BEHAVIOUR
    Tristram D. Wyatt
THE ANIMAL KINGDOM
    Peter Holland
ANIMAL RIGHTS David DeGrazia
THE ANTARCTIC Klaus Dodds
ANTHROPOCENE Erle C. Ellis
ANTISEMITISM Steven Beller
ANXIETY Daniel Freeman and
    Jason Freeman
APPLIED MATHEMATICS Alain Goriely
THE APOCRYPHAL GOSPELS
    Paul Foster

Available soon:

For more information visit our website

www.oup.com/vsi/

Ian Taylor

AFRICAN POLITICS

A Very Short Introduction

OXFORD
UNIVERSITY PRESS

OXFORD
UNIVERSITY PRESS

Great Clarendon Street, Oxford, OX2 6DP,
United Kingdom

Oxford University Press is a department of the University of Oxford.
It furthers the University's objective of excellence in research, scholarship,
and education by publishing worldwide. Oxford is a registered trade mark of
Oxford University Press in the UK and in certain other countries

Published in the United States of America by Oxford University Press
198 Madison Avenue, New York, NY 10016, United States of America

British Library Cataloguing in Publication Data

Data available

Library of Congress Control Number: 2018944718

ISBN 978–0–19–880657–8

Printed in Great Britain by
Ashford Colour Press Ltd, Gosport, Hampshire

*This book is dedicated to the memory of
James J. Hentz, Africanist scholar, gentleman,
and friend, who left us all much too early.*

Contents

List of illustrations

List of maps

Chapter 1
Introduction to Africa and its politics

Given that Africa is a continent of over a billion people, it may seem somewhat quixotic—if not arrogant—to write a book about so broad a topic as 'politics in Africa'. However, granted the rich diversity of the African experience, it is striking that continuations and themes are reflected across the continent. Questions of underdevelopment, malgovernance, and a form of political life based upon patronage are characteristic of many states in Africa. At the surface level, how politics is organized and how things *should* work through political institutions seems straightforward: all African countries have formal constitutions, bureaucracies, and symbols of the state. Yet that is not quite how politics plays out and political behaviour in Africa, while varying across the continent, is often more influenced by the personal and the informal than may be apparent to outsiders. Trying to understand this requires an understanding of the nature of most states in Africa, which are generally considered weak in capacity and, in the worst-case scenario, 'failed'. Yet these same formations are equally resilient and very good at surviving economic and political crises. Indeed, the phenomenon of the successful failed state, where the elites cling to power (often for decades) while the infrastructure of the country and the institutions of the state continue to deteriorate, is visible across Africa. 'Africa' in this book is understood to be sub-Saharan Africa, not to deny the unity of the landmass or continuities in its history, but because that is how the vast majority of the world, academic or otherwise, treats the study of the continent.

While the state is at the formalized core of African politics—and certainly generates significant resources for those who control it—how policy is decided is often opaque. The metaphor of 'veranda politics', developed by Emmanuel Terray, is here useful. The formal apparatus of government, the air-conditioned offices and conference halls, are the shop-window, put on show for dignitaries and donors. Easily visible, this realm is based on Western institutions and norms, mostly left behind by colonialism. On paper at least, they subscribe to the logic of the modern state, being technocratic and committed to democracy, development, human rights, etc. Yet this is often little more than a façade; rather, decisions are made outside of the office, out on the veranda as it were. There, patronage politics, networks, connections, and dealmaking dominates. Shared norms and expectations, understood by all participants, dictates who gets what and when, which after all is at the heart of politics everywhere. Such behind the scenes goings on should not be simply dismissed as 'corruption': this is how politics in parts of the continent operates and without understanding this, one cannot have a full sense of African politics. Those providing developmental assistance however often have assumptions wildly out of synch with what is happening on the ground. Disappointment and a sense of a lack of progress inevitably follows, with bitter recriminations on both sides.

The core questions that underpin the book are centred around issues such as how politics is typically practised on the continent; what is the nature of the state in Africa; and what accounts for Africa's underdevelopment? Underdevelopment is understood here as the increasing loss by a society over control of its own future; the emergence of structures of external dependency in the economy; net transfers of resources and national wealth to foreigners; a growing gap between the dominated and dominant nations vis-à-vis technology, life chances and living standards; consolidation of a domestic social structure whereby local elites benefit while the majority suffer; and growing social conflict as a result of the aforementioned. In the final analysis, the continent's underdevelopment explains most of the issues discussed in the book. The book will also seek to highlight how pre-colonial practices continue, as well as how colonialism affected the continent and its subsequent societies and politics. Although it is now more than sixty years since independence for most African states, the enduring effect of imperialism remains relevant. This is particularly so in how Africa is positioned in the global economy (and how that then contributes to the continent's underdevelopment) and how colonial practices changed African societies in ways that continue to reverberate today.

Africa in a nutshell

To grasp the contemporary situation in Africa, it is important to remember the following. When African states became independent, their new leaders adopted contradictory positions. On the one hand, they rejected colonialism and denounced external interference. On the other hand, a good many—the majority in fact—were very happy to continue with colonial-era institutions and policies. Capturing state power was seen as the ultimate goal, or as Kwame Nkrumah of Ghana phrased it, 'Seek ye first the political kingdom and all else shall be added unto you'. The consolidation of the state went hand in hand with the development of privileged classes who depended enormously on the government for power and accumulation. Many even strengthened ties with the former colonial powers once the imperialist flags came down. To justify their positions, most new regimes rejected parliamentary democracy and instead appealed to consensus politics. In many cases, this was self-serving and concentrated power. One-party systems became prevalent and the new leaders adopted all the trappings of the chiefly system where hierarchy and the monopolization of formal leadership was

3

practised, but minus the consensual aspect. Given that adversarial politics is the norm in democracies, numerous African leaders argued that the continent could not afford to be distracted by such divisions and instead argued that national unity was the principle, par excellence. Appeals to 'traditional African values' were often deployed. From the 1960s up until the 1990s, this form of politics was very much the norm. It was during this period that various *de facto* or *de jure* presidents-for-life emerged.

Pressure from the international financial institutions such as the World Bank and International Monetary Fund (IMF), and the end of the Cold War, alongside genuine pressures from normal Africans for change, meant that numerous African regimes were toppled or had to re-invent themselves as the entire world experienced a profound change in the early 1990s. Examples in this regard included the ending of Kenneth Kaunda's twenty-seven years in power in Zambia and Hastings Banda's thirty years as head of Malawi. This was also the era of Structural Adjustment Programmes, where economic policies designed in the West had to be implemented by recipient countries in order to qualify for new loans and assist them make repayments on older debts. It was also the era of democratization, although the two were not necessarily compatible with one another as popular resentment against the structures of free market reforms could now be expressed through the ballot box. Overall, however, the continent witnessed a decline in outright autocratic governance and, at the same time, the rise of a vibrant media and concomitant civil society. The continent today is very different from what it was when the likes of Idi Amin of Uganda and Jean-Bédel Bokassa a.k.a. Empreror Bokassa I of Central Africa ruled the roost.

However, challenges remain in terms of the continent's continued underdevelopment relative to the rest of the world and the way in which politics is practised in many parts of the continent. The structures of dependency have not radically altered and the international financial institutions and external donors still wield considerable influence in imposing policies. The continent remains exploited and its natural resources, human labour, and capital still primarily serve the interests of foreign economies, international corporations, and local ruling groups. Democratization and the flowering of public space for debate and discussion has not eradicated the dominant system of patronage politics. Vertical ties linking patron and client, often utilizing kinship or other identity networks, predominate and are generally much more important than identities constructed along class or gender lines. After experiencing the shock of democratization, many political elites across the continent re-tooled and learnt how to manipulate elections to continue business as usual. The promise of the 1990s has been dashed in a good many countries. Though clearly symptomatic of deeper problems, the type of politics practised in many states in Africa continues to be inimical to genuine nation building and broad-based, sustainable development.

Contemporary Africa's challenges

This book aims to undertake an appraisal of Africa's recent political history, examining pre-colonial political structures, the impact of colonialism, and the form and nature of post-colonial states. The African state's pre-colonial and colonial origins, which of course varied considerably, as well as the process of de-colonization and the transfer of statehood to Africans are critical here. Contemporary African states continue to be under the influence both from systems operating before the arrival of the Europeans as well as colonialism and from the subsequent adaptations those post-colonial African leaders have constructed since independence.

The key issue of Africa's persistent underdevelopment is equally crucial, as, in the final analysis, this is the key to understanding how politics in Africa is played out. What caused Africa's underdevelopment is a complex issue. Europe's past (and present) exploitation of Africa played a critical role, although it is now fashionable in some quarters to minimize this. Before the Europeans arrived, Africa had vibrant economic, social, and political structures, well-adapted societies, and political arrangements. These were, as is well-known, severely disrupted by the European colonial mission, the Arab slave trade, and the subsequent exploitation by external actors. An essentially unequal trading system was established from the mid-15th century onwards and Africa was systematically underdeveloped, as the relative per capita GDP during the colonial period, estimated by Angus Maddison, clearly attests (see Table 1).

In the 21st century, the relationship between the world and Africa continues to be primarily one of exploitation, with the active connivance of African leaders. This has allowed individual African officials to get rich, while the continent sells itself cheaply. It is a strong contention of this book that the more negative aspects of politics in Africa are but symptoms of much deeper problems, central to which is the failure by most states to promote broad-based development. There are both historical and contemporary, internal and external factors that coalesce to help explain this reality.

A number of core concepts are useful for understanding African politics, including clientelism and patronage politics, which have been touched on already. Generally speaking, much of African

Table 1. Per capita GDP, 1870–1950 (in 1990 dollars)

Country	1870	1913	1950
Western Europe	1,974	3,473	4,594
USA, Canada, Australia, New Zealand	2,431	5,257	9,288
Japan	737	1,387	1,926
Eastern Europe and ex-USSR	917	1,501	2,601
Africa	444	585	852

politics is based on personal loyalty paid to individual leaders. Common features of this form of governance include the use of coercive measures to retain power and careful management of intricate clientelistic networks. Such systems are prevalent in most states of modern Africa, where they undermine institutional capacities. Political elites that have consolidated their hold on power since independence have systematically weakened their political opponents' potential and have constructed quite complex systems of governance that retard the development of a modernized bureaucratic state as understood in the West. Ruling coalitions are relatively small and often based on identity politics (i.e. the appeal to perspectives of social groups with which people identify). The flow of revenue and resources is strictly controlled by the ruling cliques and patronage, and largesse is distributed to the various networks that underpin the system.

The social forces that currently shape contemporary politics in the continent also need to be considered: ethnicity, gender, and religion. Traditionally, African societies were based on the family, the lineage, the clan, the ethnic group, and ultimately a confederation of groups with cultural, religious, and linguistic characteristics in common. These were the units of social, economic, and political organizations and inter-communal relations. In the process of colonial state formation, these groups were divided or brought together with little or no regard to their common characteristics or distinctive attributes. They were placed in new administrative frameworks, governed by new values, new institutions, and new operational principles and techniques. The old order was incompletely replaced by the control mechanisms of capitalism. Colonialism functioned through coercive power, which ultimately rested on the police and military. National resources were extracted and exported as raw materials to feed the industries of the colonial masters and new systems undermined indigenous arrangements. Upon independence, competitions for state power and resources rapidly became winner-takes-all, utilizing diverse identities, often (but not exclusively) appealing to tribalism or religion. How such identities have been employed by the elites has been one of the great destabilizing factors in African politics.

The role of the military and how and why Africa has experienced a plethora of military coups is also of great importance. The euphoria of independence in Africa in the 1960s was quickly followed by a long succession of military coups until the late 1990s. The 2000s saw a comparative reduction, but the military still usurps political power in a number of African countries. In fact, in recent years we have seen a relative return of the men in camouflage issuing decrees over the national radio and television stations: the events in Zimbabwe in December 2017 being but one recent manifestation of this trend. Initially, military usurpation of civilian power was often stimulated by outside intervention and after the Cold War unconstitutional regime changes seemed to reduce. However, coups and 'constitutional crises' have gradually crept back into the African political sphere. How and why the military intervenes in African politics and what the military does when in power is an important theme in the study of politics in Africa.

Equally, questions about the application of various aspects of liberal democracy and electoral politics in Africa is essential. The wave of elections in Africa in the 1990s and 2000s led to the rather naive perception that democracy was triumphing across the continent. Yet it is now clear that democracy has been interpreted and applied in different ways throughout the continent, according to the whims and caprices of politicians and the ruling elites. While many African leaders lay claim to having accepted liberal democracy in theory, in reality, the majority of them are semi-democratic at best. They have allowed elections, but intrinsic democratic principles of freedom of speech, human rights, and free and transparent elections are not adhered to in many cases. Thus, even though most African states embraced elections at the end of the Cold War and these continue unevenly today, liberal democracy has not brought the expected rewards. The implications for how politics in Africa is practised are vital.

The role that Africa plays in the international system and attempts at promoting pan-continental unity is also fundamental. The global capitalist system was structured—and since then has been governed and regulated—by dominant institutions created without Africa's participation and involvement. The bulk of Africa was still under colonial subjugation when the United Nations Charter was formed in 1945, and when the Bretton Woods institutions of the World Bank and the IMF were initiated. Obviously, African interests were not taken into account and, arguably, have not been since. The Cold War's distortion of the international system coincided precisely with the moment when the majority of African states became independent. Such processes meant that for the first three or four decades of self-rule, many African leaders were given a free pass by one or other Cold War protagonist, while the distorting effects of the bipolar world proved disastrous for much of the continent. In francophone Africa, loyalty to Paris guaranteed no-questions-asked support. Both sides, the West as much as the Soviets, engaged in a cynical and manipulative game based ultimately on military contestation through proxy wars in such places as Angola and Mozambique. Not only did this lead to numerous deaths across the continent, it also left Africa awash with small arms, notably the ubiquitous AK-47, which helps contribute to high crime rates and continued de-stabilization.

Developments in the global economy however meant that by the late 1980s, Africa's situation in the international system was precarious. Saddled by huge debts and characterized by malgovernance and corruption, many African states were compelled to go through transitions that introduced varying levels of reforms. Though much of these reforms proved devastating for the average African, the liberalization of markets in many ways prepared the ground for the 2000s, when huge interest in the continent by emerging powers such as China and India propelled the continent to a re-invigorated place in the global system. China's role in particular has re-shaped and diversified the continent's international relations. Whether this has been transformative for Africa's peoples is important as, in the final analysis, how all of these processes and dynamics affect the average African is what politics in Africa is all about—or at least should be the focus of study.

Chapter 2
Pre-colonial political systems and colonialism

Pre-colonial Africa was characterized by a wide diversity of societies. Most pre-colonial societies in Africa were based on communal values, in the sense that they were autonomous units, and that members of the community took part, directly or indirectly, in the day-to-day organization of the community. Land was communally owned and could not generally be purchased or traded, although cattle and other possessions were owned personally. With a few rare exceptions (such as the pygmies in central Africa and the San of southern Africa), crop farming, at times cattle raising, and on occasion a combination of the two, supplied the means to live. African agriculture was well-adapted to the soil and weather conditions that farmers encountered. In thinly populated locations, often water-stressed, agriculture was habitually nomadic. With regard to tools, iron was employed widely, and in west Africa bronze and brass casting thrived. Well-developed agricultural systems alongside metalworking suggest that a high level of industrious activity existed. Societies must therefore have been stratified, with farmers producing sufficient food to guarantee the maintenance of skilled workers such as smiths, potters, and weavers. These in turn provided the tools, weapons, and clothing required by all. Particularly in central and southern Africa, this way of living did not generate production above subsistence levels and such economies were not concerned with amassing wealth.

Pre-colonial Africa had a wide diversity of politics and government, all related to the type of economic systems practised. Hunter-gatherers practised a form of primitive communism, while elsewhere three broad systems may be identified: large centralized kingdoms and empires; centralized mid-sized kingdoms; and widely scattered chiefdoms. Centralized kingdoms were ruled by monarchs with absolute power and were similar to their European and Asian counterparts. Mansa Musa of Mali (Figure 1), Sundiyata Keita, and Sonni Ali of the Shonghai Empire all laid claim to the divine right to kingship, as did royalty in Europe. The sovereigns managed extensive court systems where officials and vassal chiefs retained their positions in trust for the king. Such positions depended on loyalty to the monarch. Examples of such empires are the Nubians and Axumites in east Africa, Mali and Songhai in west Africa, and the Shona and Zulus in southern Africa. There was no division of powers in these systems; the king and his court exercised executive, legislative and judicial roles. Relatively complex administrations and taxation methods garnered economic resources.

1. Mansa Musa of Mali's visit to Cairo (from the Catalan Atlas, 1375).

Centralized mid-sized kingdoms were organized into city-states with structures of authority similar to the previously mentioned systems, but on a smaller scale. Indeed, the distinction between the two types of kingdom was their territorial reach. Mid-sized kingdoms were generally urbanized and the kings exercised great control. The king and a council of advisers deliberated on lawmaking, oversaw the application of laws, and mediated between petitioners. The monarch dominated access to key resources such as land and income from taxation, and commanded the army. Examples of centralized mid-sized pre-colonial polities are the Oyo and Ife kingdoms in Nigeria, the Asante in Ghana, the Buganda and Bunyoro kingdoms in Uganda, and the city-states of Benin, Mombasa and Malindi. Some of these states were renowned for their substantial towns and cities, and served as trading centres, particularly those in the Sahel. Others gained fame for their cultural and intellectual achievements, such as Timbuktu. Map 1 indicates some of the main pre-colonial kingdoms.

Finally, the widely scattered polities were acephalous communities (i.e. they did not have kings, chiefs, or obvious centralized elites) and thus were deemed 'stateless' by the colonialists when they encountered them. However, in fact such communities had well-organized governance systems. Societal norms were respected and transgressors punished. These types of political system operated at the village levels and if there was a notional leader, this post was often rotational. A strong emphasis on communal decision-making meant that wide-ranging consultations were made. In addition, leadership roles might be dispersed through village councils of elders, age grades, or secret societies. The system treasured checks and balances on the chiefs' powers, and authority was deliberately not controlled by an individual. The Setswana saying of *Kgosi ke Kgosi ka Batho* ('a chief is a chief by the people') captures the ideal. Examples of such governance systems were the Igbos in Nigeria, the Somalis, the Nuer and Dinka in South Sudan, the Maasai in Kenya and Tanzania, and the Tonga in Zambia.

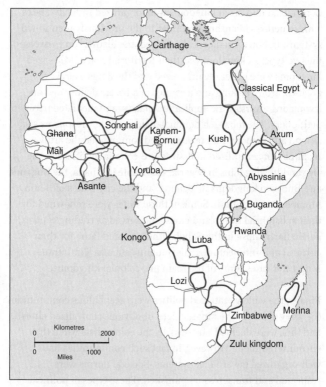

Map 1. Africa's pre-colonial kingdoms.

Irrespective of the levels of economic organization and production, and the type of governance systems in place, most influence at the local level lay in family or kinship bonds. Political and social identities were generally more related to affiliations, such as sharing a common language, than to being an inhabitant of a particular territory. Trade between coastal cities and interior regions developed, and various African peoples were brought together by shared religions, commercial ties, and military authority. Rigid demarcated borders were generally unknown.

The slave trade

Prior to the industrialized levels of slavery under the Arabs and Europeans (Figure 2), slavery took on the form of indenture whereby individuals became slaves through being prisoners of war, being indebted to a family, being kidnapped, or committing a crime. Slaves were not the property of the individual but were collectively owned by a family. The slave effectively belonged to the

2. The African slave trade.

family and became closely incorporated into it. Female slaves joined the ranks of the women, who were the main farmers in agricultural societies, and it was often the case that the child of a slave woman was born free and joined the family as an equal. The point is that before the development of the Arab and European slave trade, Africans were not engaged in the large-scale trade of selling Africans into slavery. When this did come into being, African enslavers usually captured and sold off individuals and groups belonging to other societies, thus the Asante sold captured Yorubas to the Europeans, the Amharas engaged in a slave trade of Nuers to the Arabs, etc. Animosities between groups developed as a result.

Beginning in the 15th century, the trans-Atlantic slave trade developed with Africans forcibly shipped from west, central, and eastern Africa to European colonies in the Americas. Slave trades such as the trans-Saharan, Indian Ocean, and Red Sea markets pre-dated this. According to the Trans-Atlantic Slave Trade Database, between 1525 and 1866, 12.5 million Africans were shipped to the New World, while it has been estimated that fourteen million Africans, the majority female, were sold into the Muslim world, primarily by Arabs, from the middle of the 7th century onwards (Arab enslavement of black Africans continues today in Mauritania and Sudan). By 1800, the continent's population was half of what it should have been without the slave trades. The net effect of the tragedy was to introduce ubiquitous insecurity and brutality into the affected areas, while facilitating development outside of Africa. As Eric Williams noted, the slave trade was critical in propelling the Industrial Revolution. Equally, the trade had devastating impacts on the institutional, social, and economic development of the affected societies. Antagonisms between different communities were aggravated, leading to historical mistrust which continues today. Pre-colonial institutions were disrupted, and political and social fragmentation became commonplace while local economies stagnated or became oriented towards servicing the slave trade.

It is a fact that those areas in Africa from which the most slaves had been taken are today the most impoverished. This is particularly wretched given that the parts of Africa from which the most slaves were taken were precisely the most developed prior to the slave trade. According to Nathan Nunn, if the slave trades had not occurred, then 72 per cent of the average income gap between Africa and the rest of the world would not exist today, and 99 per cent of the income gap between Africa and other developing countries would not exist. In other words, had the slave trades (and colonialism) not happened, the continent would not be the most underdeveloped region of the world. In short, the slave trade played a crucial part in the shaping of large parts of Africa, in terms not only related to levels of economic development, but also in the social and political realm. Large swathes of the continent became shambolic, open to further predations by external forces.

Colonialism

Actual colonization came late to most parts of Africa; it was not until the late 19th century that Europeans sought to actually control territory beyond some enclaves in west and southern Africa, as Map 2 indicates. Prior to this, the European presence had been confined to the coast, where complex networks of trade developed between Europeans and Africans (albeit dominated by slavery). When colonialism took place however, European rule transformed Africa forevermore. Cultural and social developments, alongside the economic sphere, were irrevocably altered, mostly negatively.

The aim of colonialism was to exploit and extract the physical, human, and economic resources of a territory to maximize the benefits for the colonizers. Those European countries which participated in this engaged in converting African economies into commodity-based trading systems whereby Africa's natural resources were exported to the metropoles for production purposes. In return, goods made in Europe were

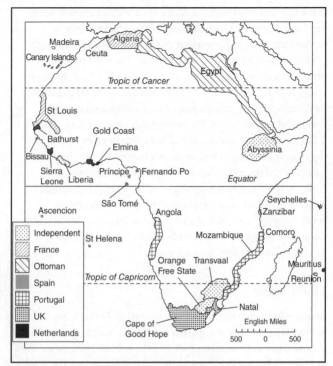

Map 2. Africa in 1870, on the eve of colonial expansion.

imported back to the colonies. The development of such economies blocked the natural development of Africa and distorted the continent into a dependent relationship with Europe where African economies became subordinated to the needs and interests of the colonizing nations. Initially a source of labour through the slave trade, as the European grip on Africa developed, the continent was misshapen in such a way that the repercussions continue today.

In 1807, the British outlawed the slave trade and 'legitimate trade' was ushered in. Africa became a valuable source of primary materials to feed a speedily industrializing Europe. Trade was typified by the widespread development of cash crops, which were traded for European merchandise. The end of the slave trade and the consequent move to the exporting of natural products from Africa integrated the continent ever more into the capitalist world economy. The so-called 'Scramble for Africa' began with King Leopold II of Belgium's assumption of control over the Congo Basin. Leopold asked for international recognition of his personal property in the Congo and, amid fears that Europeans would eventually be pitted against each other in Africa, Chancellor Otto von Bismarck of Germany initiated a conference for Europe to synchronize the land grabs. After much negotiation, Leopold was granted the Congo Free State and the principle of 'effective occupation' was established, which would recognize colonial territories in Africa. Leopold's rule subsequently led to a cruel bloodbath, which cost the lives of around ten million Congolese. For the rest of Africa, the result of the conference was the Treaty of Berlin of 1885. It is from this event that Africans in the hinterland were incorporated under European rule (albeit unevenly) and Africa's (often illogical) borders were mostly established: some 44 per cent of colonial borders were straight lines, as seen in Map 3.

The basic goal of the 'Scramble for Africa' was to deliver the maximum economic benefits to the colonizing nations at the lowest possible cost, and colonialism on a shoestring was the norm. This meant no serious efforts were made to promote the development of the inhabitants of the colonies and only a skeletal colonial state was constructed. To the colonizing nations, the requirements of their colonial subjects were rarely factored in and colonialism forced its subjects to produce almost exclusively for the export market. This logic meant that the production of specific commodities was imposed to the exclusion of the usefulness of the crop or the wider effect on the local economy and society. Thus in Tanganyika, the colonial establishment changed local agriculture from subsistence food production to the growth of cotton and sisal. In west Africa, economies

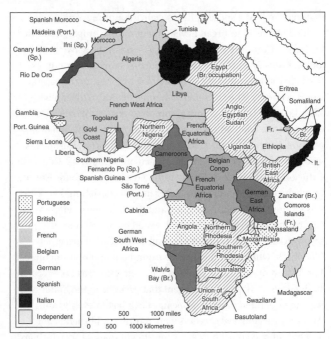

Map 3. Colonial Africa in 1914.

became centred on cocoa or groundnuts or other such cash crops. Traditional diets were transformed, as basics such as millet and sorghum became neglected. This often resulted in food insecurity.

Colonialism also sought to restrict imports into Africa to those from the colonizing nation, with exports likewise controlled. This shrank any freedom of choice in terms of what could be bought and sold. As Africans were prevented from marketing their produce freely, they were compelled to enter the economy. Local farmers were no longer able to determine what crops to cultivate: the choice was made for them by the Europeans. Intended to enrich the metropole, colonial territories were

20

required to pay the costs for their own development and management. Taxation of commerce was one key way this was achieved, with a large share of the colonial state's income being obtained from trade. This income, however, was rarely spent on the requirements of Africans, and instead was expended on infrastructure development to further facilitate exploitation. Most of the roads and rail systems built during this period were orientated towards the coast for the exportation of commodities; little or no transport links were developed between or within the colonies. Otherwise, taxation paid for the colonial bureaucracy and security—in other words, Africans paid for their own oppression.

Colonialism integrated Africa into the global economic system as it emerged in the late 19th century. Africans were incorporated, however, as unequal and dependent counterparts. The economic health of Africa became highly vulnerable to the rise and fall of commodity prices, which were themselves informed by European tastes and demands. African control over this situation was essentially non-existent. It is true that some individual Africans benefited from this process, but these were a tiny minority mainly located in coastal areas and/or servicing the needs of the colonial powers. It was from such sectors of African society, however, that the nascent tiny middle class was to emerge, with aspirations of their own which were later to lead to demands for self-rule.

Types of colonial rule

It is important to recognize that there were in fact different types of colonial rule in Africa. All for sure were based on the exploitation of the labour and resources of the continent, but the differences had an impact upon how politics was practised in different territories. One type was direct rule, mostly practised by the French and Belgians. These were centralized systems of administration based in the colonial towns, which stressed the idea of assimilation, whereby Africans could evolve into being 'civilized' and thus an *évolué*. The term 'assimilation' originated from the French word *assimiler*, which means 'to cause to resemble'. Thus, the policy of assimilation aimed at making the Africans in French colonies resemble French citizens through the dissemination of French civilization (the *mission civilisatrice*). The approach had its origins in the French Revolution, with its slogans of *liberté, égalité, fraternité*, deemed universal values. The idea, at least on paper, was that these rights should apply to anyone who was French, regardless of race. In practice, it was fundamentally racist as it elevated the mimicking of European mores as a central aspect of control. Furthermore, as the French regarded their colonies as overseas territories of France, the ultimate aim was to incorporate the colonies as extensions of France itself, rather than as distinct entities. In 1958, Charles de Gaulle indeed stated that *tous Français, de Dunkerque à Tamanrasset* ('from Dunkirk to Tamanrasset, it's all French'), the latter being deep in the Algerian south.

There were no standardized measures for determining *évolué* status, but in the Belgian and French colonies, a candidate was expected to possess fluency in French, be a Christian, and have some level of post-primary education. Politically, the effect was to divide African societies, as most *évolué*s sought after privileges unattainable to the bulk of the African populations, and actively pursued the role of go-between between the colonial administration and the natives. Indigenous African rulers were disregarded in most aspects of such governance and, in fact, policies were introduced that intentionally weakened native institutions. Notably, European civil servants were present at all levels of the colonial government, right down to local affairs. This meant that at independence, most of the territories which experienced direct rule possessed a tiny number of educated Africans, most of whom in any case saw themselves as superior and distinct from the rest of the local society.

In contrast, the British used indirect rule to manage their African colonies. This method used indigenous African rulers to supervise colonial rule, although at the highest levels of administration British bureaucrats maintained control. The policy was first popularized by Lord Lugard who served as governor of Nigeria between 1914 and 1919. Essentially, the British assumed that all Africans were organized into 'tribes', all of which possessed 'chiefs'. This was not always the case and where this was so, tribes and/or chiefs were created. Either way, as Lugard put it:

> liberty and self-development can be best secured to the native population by leaving them free to manage their own affairs through their own rulers, proportionately to their degree of advancement, under the guidance of the British staff, and subject to the laws and policy of the administration.

Those native rulers who were appointed had the responsibility to collect taxes on behalf of the British. As the key intermediaries, the chiefs were required to maintain peace and order. They also assisted in the recruitment of labour for colonial agriculture and mining interests, as well as mobilizing the people for road and railway construction. In most of British West Africa, where indirect rule was practised, 'peasant agriculture' was pursued where peasants cultivated cash crops. The obligation on the chiefs here was to supervise their subjects and ensure production.

Although less intrusive than direct rule (and also less expensive for the British), the system led to intensified inter-communal divisions *and* granted status and power to local 'big men' in a way that was unknown in most of pre-colonial Africa. Communities were rigidly divided into tribes, and this fostered disunity as each community was formally made to exist separately from others. In turn, those traditional leaders who were co-opted were often seen as collaborators who had lost the legitimacy they may once have had as rulers of the community. After all, it was the local chiefs who passed on and guaranteed policies on behalf of the colonialists. Such chiefs were largely unaccountable to the people that they ruled over, being rather responsible to the colonial power that had appointed them. Consequently, authority became something alien and thrust upon societies. This legacy of illegitimate styles of rule was to have grave consequences for post-colonial Africa. Furthermore, as colonial agents, most chiefs were inherently conservative and actually often opposed independence, as this would undermine their privileged positions. In many post-colonial states, one of the first things required for the new state was to emasculate the power of the chiefs.

A third type of colonialism was where European settlers immigrated in significant numbers. These immigrants planned to make the colonies their permanent home, but of course one where they had an elevated status. Special political and economic rights were granted in such colonies and the territory was more or less explicitly run for their benefit. Discrimination against the indigenous population was intrinsic to such colonies, as was the wholesale seizure of the best land by the settlers. Apartheid was the logical conclusion of such rule. Examples of settler colonies include Kenya and Algeria (where 1.6 million French settlers lived). The majority though were in southern Africa: South Africa, Zambia, and Zimbabwe, and the Portuguese territories of Angola and Mozambique. As the settlers had so much at stake and because the physical presence of colonial rule was greater, settler colonies were precisely those areas where the only path to independence was through violence. Thus protracted wars of liberation occurred in virtually all of the settler states, from the Mau Mau Rebellion in Kenya to the eventual election of Nelson Mandela in South Africa in 1994. Countless lives were lost in the process as Africa moved to unshackle itself from such alien rule.

Chapter 3
The transfer of power and the colonial legacy

Colonialism profoundly transformed African political, economic, and social structures. As has been pointed out, colonialism was grounded in the exploitation of the labour and natural resources of Africa for the benefit of the metropoles. For around eighty years, Europeans not only governed most of Africa (Ethiopia and Liberia being the sole exceptions), they also deprived Africans of the education necessary to manage the newly imposed economic and political systems, and, in large part, denied equal treatment to Africans. This was to have intense implications for the continent as it moved towards independence in the 1960s, as in most cases, the foundations necessary for the construction of sovereign, economically viable, and politically stable African states did not exist.

The European powers left most of their colonial possessions unprepared for self-rule, one of the worst examples being the Belgian Congo. Brussels had first discussed de-colonization in 1955 when a Belgian report reckoned that the development of a ruling elite in Congo was at least a generation behind other European colonies, and thus Congo needed at a minimum, thirty years until it was ready for independence. After rioting in the colonial capital in 1959, Brussels suddenly announced that elections for independence would be in 1960. At that point, with a population of around fifteen million people, Congo possessed no African army officers and no Congolese in the entire military with a rank higher than sergeant; only three African managers in the entire civil service; only sixteen Congolese with a university or college degree (mostly in theology); and no Congolese doctors, lawyers, or engineers. It was hardly surprising that the country, bigger in size than western Europe, quickly collapsed into anarchy (from which it has never recovered).

While perhaps the most egregious, the Belgians were hardly unique. In 1950 (i.e. seven years before independence), there were a grand total of three Africans in the colonial administrative service in what was to become Ghana. As for France, until 1946 only French citizens could be admitted to the *École Nationale de la France d'Outre-Mer*, the school for colonial bureaucrats. In 1954, six years before most of French Africa became independent, there were only two African students at the *École*. In Mozambique, not one African doctor was trained during the 500 years of Portuguese rule there.

The idea that Africans should, or even could, rule themselves was accepted only late in the day. Indeed, it was not until after the Second World War, with the massive impact this had on Europe, particularly economically, that de-colonization was really considered as an option. Developmentalism suddenly became important in colonial policy, and plans were set in store to develop a minimal social infrastructure, something that had been previously provided by missionaries. Although funds were drawn from the export of primary commodities, which was experiencing a boom in prices after the war, colonial fiscal self-sufficiency was abandoned and aid was begun to somehow kick-start 'development'. This brought with it a sudden relative expansion of the colonial state's reach, and, at the same time, stimulated expectations as to what the state was there for. Young Africans who had begun to emerge from secondary schools in large numbers in the 1950s (and universities in the 1960s) began to see government service as the natural end object of education (in any case, it was often the only job opportunity for educated Africans). The expansion of the colonial state and then Africanization to fill posts and/or replace Europeans provided huge opportunities. At the time, the consensus across Europe was that the state needed to have a strong role in the economy through nationalization. Economic planning and the institutionalization of the state in many realms of the economy was accepted as common sense and indeed promoted by the colonialists.

Importantly, the type of economies that developed under colonialism had led to the situation where intermediaries from Syria, Lebanon, and India dominated most economies outside of the colonial trading monopolies and where large-scale settler populations were absent. Colonialism had in most cases severely obstructed the evolution of an indigenous middle class and traders of foreign origin filled this gap. Missing basic industries and a sufficient infrastructure, confronted by dominant European corporations and squeezed out at the local level by foreign traders, the only resolution to the problems at hand at independence was a planned economy. However, this was without the skills, technical expertise, and funds to do so.

A hesitant developmental process was begun that was, however, too late for the rapidly growing calls for de-colonization and in many ways the Europeans were overtaken by events. African nationalism had grown rapidly after the War, influenced by the exposed myth of European supremacy. Indian independence from Britain in 1947, and French and Dutch defeats in Asia gave graphic examples that colonial rule was not forever. In particular, the defeat of the French army at Dien Bien Phu in Vietnam in 1954 was critical; the day after the battle finished, Paris announced that it was withdrawing from Indo-China. Two years later, de-colonization took on an irresistible momentum after the Suez debacle. World opinion, especially that of the United States, together with the threat of Soviet intervention, forced Britain and France to withdraw. The real locations of power in the post-war world had been unambiguously demonstrated.

It became clear that both the US and the Soviet Union opposed direct colonialism, preferring to exert their might by indirect means—ideological, economic, and military. Economic pressures were placed on the Europeans by the United States, who sought to deny Moscow the moral high ground as the Cold War deepened, as well as to open up new opportunities for American corporations. The Soviet Union for its part actively supported African independence as a means to weaken the capitalist world (alongside a genuine commitment to anti-colonialism). A war-weary public in Europe refused further sacrifices to maintain overseas colonies, and anti-colonial sentiment grew in Europe, often sympathetically linking up with the small but vociferous African agitators drawn from the middle class who demanded self-governance. Expressions of African power in the form of labour strikes, the formation of mass organizations, and the agitation of intellectuals added to the pressure.

As mentioned previously, in settler colonies bloodshed was often necessary to shift the colonialists. In Kenya, atrocities carried out by both the British and loyalist Kikuyus against Mau Mau insurgents generated a state of terror in the 1950s; while in Algeria, widespread massacres by the French military, the liberation fighters, and tit-for-tat attacks between the indigenous Algerians and the white settler population led to a death toll of around 750,000. Both countries staggered into independence in the early 1960s with these legacies. Elsewhere, the European populations held on for much longer. Table 2 indicates the progressive gaining of independence by African nations.

Where there was no large-scale settler populace, independence was less bloody, and formal power was progressively handed over to Africans. However, many of the independence days were arguably charades, where the colonial powers made a grand show of surrendering sovereignty, but where the underlying structures of control remained the same. Colonialism had been based on economic exploitation, and while African nationalist political

Table 2. Dates of independence of African countries (in chronological order of independence)

Country	Date of independence	Former power
Ethiopia (Aksum)	AD 100	–
Liberia	26 July 1847	American Colonization Society
Egypt	28 February 1922	Great Britain
South Africa	11 December 1931	Great Britain
Libya	24 December 1951	France, Great Britain—the UN
Sudan	1 January 1956	Egypt, Great Britain
Morocco	2 March 1956	France
Tunisia	20 March 1956	France
Ghana	6 March 1957	Great Britain
Guinea	2 October 1958	France
Cameroon	1 January 1960	France—UN trusteeship
Togo	27 April 1960	France—UN trusteeship
Mali	20 June 1960	France
Senegal	20 June 1960	France
Madagascar	26 June 1960	France
DRC (as Republic of Congo)	30 June 1960	Belgium
Somaliland	26 June 1960	Great Britain
Somalia (as Somali Republic, with Somaliland)	1 July 1960	Italy—UN trusteeship

(continued)

Table 2. Continued

Country	Date of independence	Former power
Benin (as Dahomey)	1 August 1960	France
Niger	3 August 1960	France
Burkina Faso (as Upper Volta)	5 August 1960	France
Côte d'Ivoire	7 August 1960	France
Chad	11 August 1960	France
CAR	13 August 1960	France
Congo-B	15 August 1960	France
Gabon	17 August 1960	France
Nigeria	1 October 1960	Great Britain
Mauritania	28 November 1960	France
Sierra Leone	27 April 1961	Great Britain
Tanganyika	9 December 1961	Great Britain
Burundi	1 July 1962	Belgium—UN trusteeship
Rwanda	1 July 1962	Belgium—UN trusteeship
Algeria	3 July 1962	France
Uganda	9 October 1962	Great Britain
Zanzibar*	10 December 1963	Great Britain—protectorate
Kenya	12 December 1963	Great Britain

Malawi	6 July 1964	Great Britain
Zambia	24 October 1964	Great Britain
The Gambia	18 February 1965	Great Britain
Botswana	30 September 1966	Great Britain
Lesotho	4 October 1966	Great Britain
Mauritius	12 March 1968	Great Britain
eSwatini (as Swaziland)	6 September 1968	Great Britain
Equatorial Guinea	12 October 1968	Spain
Guinea-Bissau	10 September 1974	Portugal
Mozambique	25 June 1975	Portugal
Cape Verde	5 July 1975	Portugal
Comoros	6 July 1975	France
São Tomé and Príncipe	12 July 1975	Portugal
Angola	11 November 1975	Portugal
Seychelles	29 June 1976	Great Britain
Djibouti	27 June 1977	France
Zimbabwe	18 April 1980	Great Britain
Namibia	21 March 1990	South Africa—UN mandate
Eritrea	24 May 1993	Ethiopia
South Sudan	9 July 2011	Sudan

The transfer of power and the colonial legacy

Note: * Merged with Tanganyika on 26 April 1964 to form the Republic of Tanganyika and Zanzibar; subsequently renamed United Republic of Tanzania on 28 October 1964. CAR = Central African Republic; Congo-B = Republic of Congo (Brazzaville); DRC = Democratic Republic of Congo.

pressure after the Second World War became irresistible, the metropoles certainly sought to protect their economic interests. To continue to benefit from Africa, the colonial powers created states which were in effect, dependencies with relatively compliant elites in place to continue business as usual. This was facilitated by the fact that many of the nationalist movements who argued for independence were merely asking that foreign domination in the bureaucratic posts be ended; the actual economic and political structures of domination were rarely questioned, and were, in fact, eagerly assumed by a new, indigenous clique.

Furthermore, at the international level, when the new African states were admitted into the global system, they did so at the lowest levels of the global hierarchy. In effect, the de-colonization process created a large number of the world's most artificial states, with very weak internal legitimacy and economic bases that were, in the main, not conducive to nation building. In addition, when the Organization of African Unity (OAU) recognized the principle of the inviolability of the existing colonial borders at its formation in 1963, it was evident that the de-colonization struggle was limited within certain parameters. Very few African leaders sought to challenge this reality and those that did, such as Kwame Nkrumah of Ghana and Patrice Lumumba of Congo (Figure 3), were quickly dispatched: Lumumba being assassinated in 1961 and Nkrumah being overthrown by a coup in 1966.

Unfortunately for the continent, de-colonization took place at the height of the Cold War. This encouraged ideological puppets and effective satellite states, where what mattered was not the domestic structures of power and the requirements of society, but rather to which camp did a particular African state subscribe. Political accountability and the opinions of the populations concerned were irrelevant. Such dynamics quickly led to the emergence of dictatorships who were emboldened by unconditional support from external allies. At the same time, parts of Africa became the terrain for various proxy wars

3. Arrest/capture of Patrice Lumumba of Congo.

sponsored by the two superpowers. The net result was the proliferation of huge amounts of weapons across the continent, the destruction of already threadbare infrastructure, and the death and displacement of millions of Africans. There *were* attempts to navigate around the dualistic option of either/or through such initiatives as the Non-Aligned Movement (NAM), and a number of leaders such as Julius Nyerere of Tanzania and Kenneth Kaunda of Zambia were sincere in trying to avoid Africa being drawn into the superpower confrontation. However, the reality was that most African leaders opted for one side or the other, either implicitly or explicitly. Overall, the default position though was to maintain varying degrees of warm relations with the West and, in particular, the former colonial power.

Only a few countries opted for the Soviet side, namely Angola, Benin, Cape Verde, Congo-B, Guinea, Guinea-Bissau, Madagascar, Mozambique, and Seychelles. Ethiopia and Somalia actually

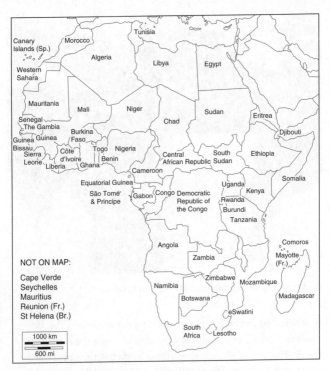

Map 4. Post-colonial Africa.

switched sides in the mid-1970s, with formerly monarchical
Addis Ababa becoming the capital of Soviet intentions in Africa
after Haile Selassie's overthrow. Cold War dynamics seriously
distorted African politics across the continent, further
complicating the ability of the new countries to challenge the
legacy of colonialism which they had inherited (Map 4).

The legacy of colonialism

The legacies of colonialism live on today in myriad forms. The key
legacy is economic, which massively influences the political realm.

The root problem of Africa's lacklustre economic performance since independence lies in the asymmetry between the role of the continent in the global economy and the way in the world has penetrated Africa. Broadly speaking, the inflexibility of the global system has largely prevented African economies from breaking out of their role as primary producers. Reasons for this would include continuing weak infrastructure; a lack of access to technology; the entrenched position of industrialized nations; the limitations of most African domestic markets; and policies in the North that prevent African manufacturers from entering foreign markets.

As has been noted, during the colonial period (and after), the composition of Africa's foreign trade was primarily decided by the requirements of the metropoles. As has been mentioned, African countries mainly export natural resources and import manufactured goods, and this structure of trade has not been meaningfully transformed since independence. The result has been that there is a contradiction between production and consumption patterns, what Issa Shivji terms 'structural disarticulation', where Africa exhibits a 'disarticulation between the structure of production and the structure of consumption. What is produced is not consumed and what is consumed is not produced.' This incongruity has served as a key factor behind the continent's underdevelopment and hugely informs the political economy of most African countries. This is the chief legacy of colonial rule and is displayed in the three main exports, with their share in total exports of individual African countries (see Table 3).

In terms of governance, many African states are considered weak, in the sense that their capacity to deliver public goods is poor. This weakness is a result of legacies bequeathed by colonialism and then hugely compounded by poor governance. As has been mentioned, colonialism made very little effort to develop Africa or the colonial state, and thus at independence, most new governments found themselves with states with inadequate

Table 3. Top three exports for African countries

Country	Product I (%)	Product II (%)	Product III (%)
Algeria	Petroleum (40.0)	Natural gas (15.3)	Light oils (12.1)
Angola	Petroleum (96.0)		
Benin	Petroleum (40.1)	Light oils (13.6)	Cotton (9.6)
Botswana	Diamonds (72.9)	Processed diamonds (8.0)	Nickel (6.4)
Burkina Faso	Gold (65.2)	Cotton (19.8)	
Burundi	Coffee (46.1)	Tea (17.3)	Tantalum (6.9)
Cameroon	Tuna (23.0)	Mackerel (14.6)	Other fish (13.8)
Cape Verde	Petroleum (50.1)	Cocoa (11.4)	Wood (6.7)
CAR	Wood (60.8)	Cotton (20.6)	
Chad	Petroleum (95.2)		
Comoros	Cloves (53.4)	Vanilla (14.5)	Ships for breaking up (12.6)
Congo-B	Petroleum (78.9)	Copper (9.9)	
Côte d'Ivoire	Cocoa (47.1)		
Djibouti	Charcoal (16.2)	Coffee (14.7)	Sesame (6.5)
DRC	Cathodes (37.6)	Copper (22.1)	Petroleum (16.8)
Equatorial Guinea	Petroleum (68.2)	Natural gas (23.5)	

Eritrea	Copper (93.7)		
Ethiopia	Sesame (24.7)	Coffee (24.2)	Cut flowers (9.8)
Gabon	Petroleum (81.3)	Manganese (8.5)	
The Gambia	Cashews (36.6)	Wood (27.6)	Groundnuts (5.0)
Ghana	Petroleum (32.5)	Cocoa (19.8)	Gold (19.7)
Guinea	Petroleum (40.4)	Aluminium (35.6)	Gold (10.8)
Guinea-Bissau	Cashews (75.0)	Wood (19.8)	
Kenya	Tea (15.9)	Cut flowers (11.5)	Petroleum (8.1)
Lesotho	Diamonds (40.2)	Clothes (17.1)	
Liberia	Iron (40.7)	Ships (13.9)	Rubber (12.9)
Madagascar	Nickel (24.0)	Vanilla (9.1)	Cloves (4.7)
Malawi	Tobacco (59.7)	Tea (8.0)	Sugar (6.2)
Mali	Cotton (43.0)	Gold (34.2)	Sesame (6.2)
Mauritania	Iron (42.4)	Gold (11.4)	Octopus (7.3)
Mauritius	Fish (13.8)	Sugar (9.3)	Clothes (6.8)
Mozambique	Aluminium (20.7)	Precious stones (16.8)	Light oils (8.8)
Namibia	Diamonds (28.0)	Zinc (13.7)	Fish (6.8)
Niger	Light oils (32.3)	Petroleum (19.7)	Sesame (16.2)
Nigeria	Petroleum (81.4)	Natural gas (12.3)	

(*continued*)

Table 3. Continued

Country	Product I (%)	Product II (%)	Product III (%)
Rwanda	Tantalum (27.0)	Tin (19.8)	Coffee (15.5)
São Tomé and Príncipe	Cocoa (61.2)	Ships for breaking up (13.3)	Chemicals (5.6)
Senegal	Gold (16.8)	Fish (10.3)	Phosphoric acid (7.3)
Seychelles	Tuna (72.9)		
Sierra Leone	Iron (76.8)	Diamonds (8.1)	
Somalia	Sesame (29.0)	Goats (24.2)	Camels (22.8)
South Africa	Gold (8.9)	Iron (6.1)	Platinum (5.5)
South Sudan	Petroleum (99.8)		
Sudan	Petroleum (66.1)	Sesame (7.7)	
eSwatini	Drink concentrates (24.3)	Sugar (15.1)	Chemicals (10.8)
Tanzania	Gold (15.5)	Tobacco (10.3)	Sesame (6.5)
Togo	Gold (24.6)	Petroleum (18.2)	Electrical energy (6.2)
Uganda	Coffee (30.1)	Sesame (6.3)	Cement (5.5)
Zambia	Copper (59.7)	Tobacco (5.8)	
Zimbabwe	Tobacco (39.9)	Chrome (10.9)	Sugar (6.9)

Notes: CAR = Central African Republic; Congo-B = Republic of Congo; DRC = Democratic Republic of Congo.

Source: World Bank, 'World Integrated Trade Solution' (https://wits.worldbank.org).

control over their territories outside of the urban centres. The weak political base of the new African countries meant that they were hampered from the start.

African nationalist movements had been relatively late in developing, and when they assumed power, they encountered artificial states enclosed by often irrational borders and a weak sense of nationhood. The new ruling classes that emerged were mainly from the urbanized small middle classes. Capitalism in the form of colonialism had not acted as the transformative agent in Africa that it had in Europe, in altering societal relations and freeing up the economy. In Europe, the replacement of rural and craft economies by the Industrial Revolution increased productive capacity through the growth of factories and a mass urbanized working class, yet in Africa, while local craft industries were destroyed, commerce was not fostered beyond cash crops and mineral extraction. What African labour that was involved in such production was limited to mostly unskilled, poorly paid positions.

Consequently, with very few exceptions (primarily in southern Africa), the working class was minimal and played no serious part in post-independence politics. Instead, the nascent middle class played the key political role in providing leadership. The consequence of this was that while passing themselves off as representing the interests of all Africans, their material interests often aligned with the metropole's. The contradiction between the educated nationalists and the colonial powers was not particularly deep, and so acting as intermediaries and gatekeepers between their economies and the global system became the new leaders' key function. Such actors had little interest in, and did not feel accountable to, the rural population. The net result was that in those African states where little effort was made to confront the colonial legacy, the hierarchy of the home-grown state machinery, from chiefs to village headmen or -women, remained after independence, while in those African states that sought to alter the governance system, a centralized despotic system generally emerged. District- and local-level heads were retained on an appointed and unelected basis, answerable only to the new state. In some countries, such as Kenya, colonial-era laws were preserved to uphold the legal basis for such systems of governance.

Of course, different ideological visions for independent Africa emerged at the time of independence. Although the majority of new rulers favoured a continuation of extant economic and political relations with the metropoles (albeit with new flags and anthems), there were leaders who did advocate real independence, continental unity, and left-leaning policies regarding state-led development. Leaders of this ilk, such as Nkrumah, Nyerere, Sékou Touré of Guinea, and (later) Thomas Sankara of Burkina Faso were inclined to draw their support from trade unions, students, and intellectuals. Reflecting on the problems ahead, Nkrumah early on recognized the tensions between the two types of post-colonial leadership:

> In the dynamics of national revolution there are usually two local elements: the moderates of the professional and 'aristocratic' class and the so-called extremists of the mass movement...The moderates are prepared to leave the main areas of sovereignty to the colonial power, in return for a promise of economic aid. The so-called extremists are men who do not necessarily believe in violence but who demand immediate self-government and complete independence. They are men who are concerned with the interests of their people and who know that those interests can be served only by their own local leaders and not by the colonial power.

Given the dire state of most states and economies at independence, as well as the consensus around state-led development, it is unsurprising that most new African states initially pursued nationalization and directed economic growth with the state in charge. As John Saul and Colin Leys noted:

> At independence—between 1955 and 1965—the structural weaknesses of Africa's economic position were generally recognised and it was assumed on all sides that active state intervention would be necessary to overcome them. Although Africa would still be expected to earn its way by playing its traditional role of primary-product exporter, the 'developmental state' was to accumulate surpluses from the agricultural sector and apply them to the infrastructural and other requirements of import-substitution-driven industrialisation.

It should be pointed out here that, initially, many African countries experienced strong economic growth and levels of development (roughly from 1960 to 1975). The relative employment share of manufacturing during this period almost doubled, as did the manufacturing value added share. The initiation of economies of scale, the application of new technologies, and other developments meant that this was the golden age of Africa's growth performance. An emphasis on state investment and national development was based on import-substitution industrialization (i.e. diversifying domestic production so as to reduce the dependence on foreign imports). Such policies required the central mobilization of capital, planning, and management from above. The state during this period expanded considerably, something that was necessary given the state in which the colonialists had left Africa and the tasks regarding national development. However, problems remained and grew as the continent moved forward. In practice, there were few attempts to negotiate the relationship between the metropoles and their former colonial possessions and efforts that were made were sabotaged by Western hostility.

Attempts at autonomous national development had to face up to the fact that mass poverty, underdevelopment, and often-grotesque levels of inequality could not be resolved overnight. In some countries, the sheer size and scale of capital resources required to address the legacies of colonialism were not present. In addition, Western powers endeavoured to guarantee that African nations could not create the foundations for economic independence. Interference intended to undermine development was manifested in European policies to extend and reinforce unfavourable trade policies inherited from the colonial period to restricting foreign investment to areas of an African country's economy that would directly expedite extraction. Indeed, maintaining Africa in a dependent position to the West was systematically pursued, something facilitated in numerous countries by compliant African leaders. These new elites took for granted that they should be leaders and it became apparent that many deemed it unthinkable that they could be replaced or even challenged. If the clique in power had led the country to independence, an often chronically personalized system of control developed where self-styled 'Fathers of the Nation' saw themselves as standing in the same relationship to their citizens as a father does to his children.

The lack of development inherited from colonialism was also used by the new elites to justify 'unity' and one-party states, often with reference to the idea that the country was either too poor or too busy to have to deal with 'politics'. As Kwame Nkrumah stated, 'At the present stage of Ghana's economic development the whole community must act in the national interest.' State and nation building encouraged the centralization of power and the creation of political monopolies. Particularly in ethnically or religiously divided new states, the elimination of political competition was seen as a 'necessary device' for the management of societal divisions and the eradication of 'tribalism'. However, whatever the specific construction of the immediate post-colonial state in Africa, the vast majority rapidly became interventionist but inefficient states which lacked the human capital necessary to manage a modern economy. The new states effectively strangled the (already underdeveloped and dependent) economy within a context of autocracy where societal divisions and stark levels of poverty and inequality called the state's very legitimacy into question. The legacies of political segregations, race discriminations, and colonial definitions and divisions combined with the legacy of economic plunder and the distorting effects of the Cold War, alongside a global economic system rigged in favour of the West. All of this joined together to create a hostile environment for Africa's post-colonial trajectory.

Chapter 4
The primacy of patronage politics

In talking about something as broad as 'African politics', generalizations are necessary, and the applicability of concepts to individual African countries is conditional. Having said that, it cannot be denied that a large number of post-colonial African countries, bounded by formal frontiers and with an international presence at various international institutions such as the United Nations, function quite differently from conventional understandings of what a formal state is and should do. This is of course, not surprising, but in order to understand politics on this continent, the concept of neo-patrimonialism has largely become the standard tool of analysis.

In formal bureaucratic states, authority is distributed in a fixed way as 'official duties' while power is strictly delimited by rules and regulations. Furthermore, ideally, only qualified persons are employed in the civil service, and 'connections' should not be a part of the hiring process. These three elements constitute bureaucratic authority and are the underpinnings of the modern state, at least in theory. Hierarchy and levels of grades of authority exist, obviously, but such systems allow the decisions of a lower office to be appealed to a higher authority in a regulated manner. Civil servants are separated from their private life; and public monies and equipment are divorced from the private property of the official. Rules are more or less stable and are public, and bureaucrats are supposed to be impartial and may not favour relatives, friends, etc. This type of state is, however, very recent. It developed alongside capitalism and the requirements for an orderly state to regulate and protect the interests of the capitalist class. Prior to modern states, the norm was gerontocracy (i.e. rule by the elders), patriarchalism (i.e. absolute power for the king on a kinship basis being the monarch's personal prerogative), and patrimonialism (where power was arbitrary and administration of a wider population was under the direct control of the ruler). Indeed, patrimonialism was a social order where patrons secured the loyalty and support of clients by bestowing benefits to them from state resources. This might be best summed up by Louis XIV of France's view of power with his phrase *l'état, c'est moi.*

Neo-patrimonialism

The prefix 'neo' indicates a novel version of patrimonialism. Neo-patrimonialism in short is where patronage, clientelism, rent-seeking, etc., exist but where the structures of a modern state are also in place. Here, clientelism is understood as the exchange of specific services and resources; and rent-seeking, where an individual or group receives resources from another person or persons as the result of a 'favourable' decision on some public policy (such as allowing an oil company to operate in a state's territory in exchange for payment). The system rests on well-understood, if unequal, reciprocity; while the operation of political institutions and policy (ideally impersonal in the modern state) is instead largely influenced by the exercise of personalized power. This is the 'veranda politics' that has been previously mentioned. Under neo-patrimonial systems, the separation of the public from the private is recognized (even if only on paper) and it is certainly publicly displayed through observable displays of the modern state—a flag, a government, and a bureaucracy, etc. However, in practical terms, the private and public spheres are customarily not detached, and the external appearances of statehood are often façades hiding the real workings of the system.

In many African countries, the state bureaucracies inherited from the colonial period, however weak and ineffective they were, have become even more dysfunctional and severely constrained in their officially stated duties. Indeed, personnel within many state bureaucracies have tended to develop their own set of interests. At the individual level, the primary concern is ensuring job security and prosperity for oneself and one's dependants. In such a context, the dominant logic that ensues further distorts the civil servant's role away from the ideal bureaucrat, who is meant to be loyal to the state, rather than the regime currently in power. Furthermore, numerous African bureaucracies are staffed with often desperate individuals who are under pressure from a variety of angles (e.g. family, clients, patrons) to continue either to earn money or to act as a gatekeeper to some segment of the state's resources. Sharing the largesse that may accrue from a formal position in the state is expected and deemed the duty of the person who holds this post. Those who have the opportunity are expected to use the power and resources at their disposal and failure to do so will likely result in bitter opprobrium from those expecting to benefit from the situation.

In general, post-colonial African leaders have relied on coercive control and patronage through capturing power over the state, rather than through constructing a functioning impartial administration. While, of course, clientelism and patronage are *not* unique to Africa, the type of intensive neo-patrimonialism that we can observe across large swathes of the continent is indeed noteworthy. Such regimes may be said to exhibit four characteristics. First, they practise clientelism to obtain and maintain political support. Political authority is centred on the giving and gaining of favours in a series of exchanges that go from the village level up to the president. Practices of patronage might be personal favours, such as appointments to important government posts, but often include more mundane exercises such as paying individuals' or communities' school fees, electricity and water bills, or distributing tools, seeds, and fertilizers for agriculture. The outright handing out of cash is also popular, usually with the (false) implication that the patron is personally distributing his or her own money, rather than funds misappropriated from the state.

Second, this clientelism is based on access to state resources, controlled by leaders abiding by a strict logic. As a result, the boundary between the public and private spheres is extremely blurred. Within this context, the third characteristic is the centralization of power, usually around the presidency, which, in turn, is usually located within the capital city. Finally, neo-patrimonial states are hybrid regimes, wherein informal mechanisms of political authority coexist with the formal trappings of the modern state. These regimes are hybrids because the governing elites rely upon the accoutrements of a state, even as they consistently subvert it for their own advantage. Daily, government in a neo-patrimonial regime resembles a balancing act to maintain a degree of political stability by satisfying the regime's supporters and weakening its opponents.

Crucially, resources extracted from the state or the economy are deployed as the means to maintain support and legitimacy, with the concomitant effect that the control of the state is equivalent to the control of resources, which in turn is crucial for remaining a 'big man' (and mostly it is a man and not a woman, see Chapter 5). The big man syndrome is a quasi-traditional set of paternalistic practices, which elevate an individual over others. Many African elites believe they are the only ones destined to rule and feel above the law, which is only for the 'little people', the ordinary citizens and not the big man. Control of the state serves the twin purposes of lubricating patronage networks *and* satisfying the selfish desire of elites to self-enrich themselves, in many cases in a quite spectacular fashion. Big men use wealth (often secured illicitly) to show that they are more of a magnanimous father figure than their opponents are. As Ahmadou Kourouma wryly notes in his fictitious treatment of an African president:

> [The president] must appear to be the wealthiest man in the land. There is no future, no influence to be had in independent Africa for he who wields supreme executive power if he does not parade the fact that he is the richest and most generous man in his country. A true, great African leader gives gifts, ceaselessly, every day.

Such situations help explain the profound reluctance by African presidents to hand over power voluntarily, and why very many African regimes end messily, often in coups. In most cases the democratic option is either absent or is not respected by the loser—the stakes simply are too high, as once one is out of the loop vis-à-vis access to state resources, the continuation of one's status as a big man and the ability to enrich oneself becomes virtually impossible. Politics in Africa thus tends to be a zero-sum game.

Explaining the phenomenon

In most African countries, the economy is undiversified and access to major resources for most depends upon being inside the state apparatus. Subsequently, patrons reward supporters with sinecures in the government and bureaucracies are organizations in which staff are less agents of state policy than proprietors, distributors, and even significant consumers of the authority and resources of the state. Handing out bureaucratic posts has become an important way in which leaders can secure support. Clientelism is central to neo-patrimonialism, with widespread networks of clients receiving services and resources in return for support. This is well-understood and even expected in many African countries. Indeed, the exercise of personalized exchange, clientelism, and corruption may be internalized. In some countries it is considered normal to steal state funds if the opportunity arises, especially if these are then used to benefit not only the individual but also members of his or her community. This is called prebendalism. Such practices may be condemned only as far as they advantage someone else or other communities, rather than oneself and one's own group.

In thinking why this may be the case, the work of the Nigerian political scientist Peter Ekeh is very helpful. Ekeh referred to two public realms, which he called the primordial and the civic public. These two spheres exhibit different rights and citizenship obligations and, though linked, have different standards of morality. This is primarily because the state that was left by colonialism possessed minimal legitimacy and was not embedded in African communities for a long enough time to transform African society. Thus, colonialism left two public realms: the native sector and the modern public sector. In the primordial sector, morality is highly regarded but this area has no real economic reward; it is used rather to gain respect and security. In contrast, the civic public realm is purely for economic gain. It is an imported alien system based on unfamiliar values and crystallized in the Western state structure. This realm is amoral; one is not obligated to give back. Ekeh argued that Africans are members of the two publics and will use the civic public realm for gain if possible, so that they may give to their communities and gain respect. In such circumstances, it is moral and legitimate to be what Westerners would term 'corrupt', in order for one to strengthen one's position in the primordial public. These two publics together form African citizenship and create a disputed sense of what constitutes a good citizen.

National development and a broad-based productive economy is far less a concern to elites within such systems than the continuation of the gainful utilization of resources for the individual advantage of the ruler and his or her clientelistic networks. At the same time, the bureaucracy has developed its own set of interests (personal survival) and logic as organizations that further distort their role away from the ideal modern state and more towards a loose set of skeleton institutions lacking in most capacities other than to act as predators upon the population or gatekeepers to resources. Such an environment has had the effect of creating a whole swathe of politically connected persons who are dependent upon largesse from state elites and who act as a support constituency, while mediating between the big men or women at the top and the masses below. In such circumstances, the state has become ever more predatory.

One of the fundamental problems with such systems is that they breed great resentment in individuals and groups that are excluded and hence are denied access to resources. It is in this sense that the ruling classes in many African states lack consensual rule over society. By the ruling class, we mean the senior political elites and bureaucrats, the leading members of commerce, the nascent middle class, and the top members of the security arms of the state. The early years of post-colonial nationalism in Africa were, broadly speaking, an attempt to build a state project which bound society together around more issues than simply discontent with the imperialist powers. This project however quickly collapsed into autocracy, particularly as economic conditions deteriorated sharply after the oil crisis of the mid-1970s. As the ruling elites were unable to preside over a state that was viewed with any shred of legitimacy by the majority of society, they reverted to other systems of governance to dominate opponents and gather support. These were commonly expressed through both the threat and actual use of violence and the immediate disbursal of material benefits to supporters within the context of neo-patrimonial regimes. Without these twin strategies, both generally unfavourable to long-term development and political stability, the ruling elites in many African countries cannot maintain order. A clear pattern of leadership emerged, which merely serves the narrow interests of the ruling elites, who, in the meantime, exhibit a scornful disregard for the basic needs and interests of ordinary African citizens.

This sort of political culture has had important consequences for Africa, not least a deeply negative impact on the overall security environment. In particular, it has encouraged civil conflict and many attempts to overthrow incumbent regimes. The modes of governance in many African countries have also encouraged despotism and unpredictability, the latter of course being anathema to the construction of a stable order and broad-based development. As a result, for most of the post-colonial period, much of Africa has been trapped in a cycle of societal conflict, both at the extreme level of the wars in Liberia or Sierra Leone and at the more mundane juncture where states stagger from one crisis to another. The political story of a variety of African states can be interpreted as revolving around a struggle for power and survival that has marginalized all other concerns. Of course, at the root of all this is the continent's underdevelopment.

Indeed, building a project that encompasses national development and a broad-based productive economy is a low priority for many African elites. Instead, more effort is directed to ensuring the continuation of a system that permits the gainful use of resources for the individual advantage of the ruler and his or her clientelistic networks. As Bertrand Badie explains:

> On the one hand, economic development is a goal that every head of state must pursue...On the other hand, an overly active policy of development risks producing several negative results: it would valorize the competence of the technocratic elite relative to that of the fragile political elite, break up social spaces and favour the constitution of a civil society capable of counterbalancing the political system, and indeed, neutralize neo-patrimonial strategies.

Such tendencies are particularly problematic in resource-rich countries in Africa.

The extractive state

Colonialism inserted Africa into the world economy, in the main, as enclave economies dependent upon one or two commodities or minerals. An enclave economy is an economy that exports extractive products that are concentrated in relatively small geographic areas. The mines of Shaba province in the Congo, the rubber plantations of Liberia, and the copper mines of Zambia are good examples. What this means is that revenue generation is physically confined to small locales, with the prime markets for the products being external. This makes the general economic condition of geographic areas beyond the enclave subordinate, if not irrelevant, to those in power. In such circumstances, the idea that resources should rather be channelled towards 'national development' is, in the main, not on the agenda as wealth generation and survival does not depend on productive development, but is dependent upon control over select areas of the country (i.e. where the mines and plantations are) or by the manipulation of the market for personal reasons of power and profit.

Unfortunately for Africa, access to rents to distribute to patronage networks and thus retain key support can be based on the capture of relatively limited geographic areas. In other words, investment in infrastructure and the advancement of policies that brings in revenue for the elites but that also benefit broad swathes of the population (such as agricultural policies that encompass large sections of the community) is not required. Resource-rich countries with enclave economies do not actually require functioning states or a developed national infrastructure to generate revenues for those in power. Numerous examples, such as Angola, the two Congos, Equatorial Guinea, Liberia, Nigeria, and Sierra Leone attest to this reality.

States that have managed to relatively avoid such negative effects are those where the elites do not simply rely on enclave production for their revenues. Senegal, with its embedded export crop production that encompasses large segments of the population, is one example, while Botswana, with an elite rooted in cattle ownership and beef exports (which needs infrastructure and

4. Oil well in Nigeria.

investment), is another, albeit one that also possesses features of
an enclave economy with its diamond industry. Neither country is
free of patronage politics, but neither are simply based on efforts
to create and sustain rent-seeking opportunities for the elites.
South Africa, with its diversified and relatively mature capitalist
economy, is another example. But, these examples aside, broadly
speaking the net effect at the political level of the nature of
personal rule has been to erode any sense of broad public
accountability beyond the immediate networks (Figure 4).

Summary remarks

Africa's developmental predicament has remained due to the
combination of historical factors (the colonial legacy), the
structure of the global system, and that fact that many African
leaders have fallen short of executing thoroughgoing economic
and political reforms and overseeing capable administrative
states. This is because, be they actual presidents or powerful
bureaucrats, the continent's leaders have continued with
clientelistic politics which safeguard their advantaged positions

within society and provide access to resources, even while development remains trapped and the broad masses suffer. There is little evidence that this situation is fundamentally changing; the political terrain of many African countries is dominated by a narrow group of elites who have been at the apex of the system for years, often since independence.

The logic of politics in many African countries is that its operations are largely based on and directed by the imperatives of patronage. Long-term development and broad-based inclusivity is more or less off the agenda in many countries. While one needs to be fully aware of the structural constraints, the history of post-colonial Africa has sufficiently demonstrated that harmful exogenous influences work alongside the destructive talents of home-grown elites and that simultaneous economic and political change on the continent is exceedingly complex and difficult.

Here of course, the diversity of Africa needs emphasizing; not all African states fit all of the characteristics outlined previously. In some countries, there is a high to medium separation of the public and the private, a form of bureaucratic neo-patrimonialism with a relatively strong state with a functioning civil service monopolizing power via formalized state structures. Examples would include Ethiopia, Eritrea, Tanzania, and Senegal. Elsewhere, political systems may exhibit medium to low separation of the public-private distinction, with the existence of a wide strata of oligarchic rent-seeking actors, acting together with or in place of governmental institutions, primarily through networks of patronage. Examples here would include Nigeria, Cameroon, Zambia, and, in fact, most of Africa. Finally, there are the extreme forms of patronage politics, sultanistic neo-patrimonial regimes where there is a minimal separation of the public and private domain. In such regimes, an extreme concentration of power around the president is evident and the system is almost pure personal rulership. Examples here would be the two Congos, Zimbabwe, Angola, Gabon, eSwatini, and Equatorial Guinea.

There are also examples of African countries that do not really fit the neo-patrimonial model. States such as Botswana, Mauritius, Cape Verde, and *possibly* Rwanda, South Africa, Namibia (and, to a lesser extent, Ghana and Seychelles) would be placed somewhere in between the bureaucratic neo-patrimonial pattern and the modern Western state model. Countries may also move from one broad type to another. For instance, under Sani Abacha (1993–8), Nigeria was a sultanistic regime with astounding levels of corruption and a highly personalized system of governance. Nigeria today is now probably on the border between that and the oligarchic model, although it should be emphasized that such categorizations are by no means a precise science.

Yet in general terms, many of Africa's leaders, even though they routinely denounce corruption and tribalism, maintain informal networks that are the basis of their power and which are fundamentally corrupt in the Western sense and exacerbate societal tensions vis-à-vis those outside of the patronage loops. The quest for legitimacy in the primordial public, as Ekeh avers, requires the fulfilment of obligations that have nothing to do with the emergence of a 'neutral' civic public sphere in the form of a modern state. Instead, this is exercised through links based on relationships such as friendship, kinship, regional, or ethnic relations. Politics then is characterized by the existence of formal institutions (however dysfunctional) and elite commitment (however rhetorical) to the separation of public and private spheres, even while informal norms flourish. The political culture and logic is thus one of a mixture of formal and informal institutions, rules, norms, and practices, with personalism, clientelism, and patronage granting legitimacy in a winner-takes-all milieu. All of this is based on fluid political alliances grounded in the pursuit of power (and money) rather than on issues of political principles or ideologies. African leaders control the state, but it is a state that their own practices daily undermine.

Chapter 5
Women in African politics

Gender inequality on the continent varies depending on each community's histories, culture, colonial legacy, and levels of economic development. However, taken as a whole, inequality is very real and has a direct impact upon the possibilities of the active involvement of women in political processes in Africa. A direct result of such inequalities is that while in some countries the majority of voters are female, those who hold authority and power, and those who are elected to positions within the state, are largely men. To date, very few women have held the position of being head of state *and* of the government, which is where real power lies, as indicated in Table 4. It should be noted that Ruth Perry was chairperson of the Council of State when there was, in fact, no effective Liberian state in existence due to civil war.

Political participation is vital to a well-functioning democracy of whatever type. In most parts of the world (including in the West), women are underrepresented and men dominate decision-making levels. In Africa this is no less true, and in some countries exclusion based on gender means that women are marginalized from many political processes. It should be noted that there are, however, anomalies such as Rwanda, which leads the world in terms of gender representation, and where over 60 per cent of parliamentarians are women. In general though, women are often sidelined and society is structurally gendered on unequal terms.

Table 4. Female African heads of state and government

Name	Country	Office	Start	End	Length of term
Ruth Perry	Liberia	Chair, Council of State	3 September 1996	2 August 1997	333 days
Ellen Johnson-Sirleaf	Liberia	President	16 January 2006	22 January 2018	12 years, 6 days
Ivy Matsepe-Casaburri	South Africa	Acting President	24 September 2008	25 September 2008	14 hours
Joyce Banda	Malawi	President	7 April 2012	31 May 2014	2 years, 54 days

For instance, African women hold 66 per cent of all jobs in the non-agricultural informal sector but only make 70 cents for each dollar made by men.

There is in fact a high economic cost for Africa when women are not more fully integrated into national economies. Gender inequality in the labour market alone is estimated to have cost sub-Saharan Africa about $95 billion annually between 2010 and 2014. The explanation for the obvious gender disparities in Africa is located in the cultural and social traditions, themselves deeply affected by economic, political, and ideological aspects of Africa's trajectory both pre- and post-colonial. While it is true that African women have always been active in agriculture, trade, and other economic pursuits, certain gender roles have changed over time and this has affected the role of women in formal political processes.

The pre-colonial situation

The pre-colonial era was a period when there were wide-ranging variations in African political systems. Differences existed between hunter-gatherers and agricultural societies, between centralized and non-centralized systems, and between formal office holding and informal domestic or community power. These differences notwithstanding, inequality between genders in Africa did not permanently favour men before the European incursions. In numerous communities, women functioned as the queen or queen mother, participating in society's governance and acting as a mentor to the male chief. Indigenous structures commonly permitted women to organize their own public business without undue meddling from men; in some case, dual systems broken down along gender lines existed. Traditional healers, many of them women, also played substantial roles. Through birth and care of children, some women developed extensive knowledge of herbs and healing powers, and this often meant that they played important religious roles. In Cameroon, for example, the Takembeng social movement, according to oral tradition, enjoyed mystical powers drawn from women's reproductive roles and performed ostracizing rituals against individuals in their communities. The potency of such power continues today, with Takembeng women often leading protest marches.

In contrast to the broad effect of the introduction of capitalism into Africa, pre-colonial wives in many societies were not fully dependent upon their husbands and could often turn to age-grade associations and leaders with some degree of power. Households were economic units with shared responsibilities and female contributions to the household as farmers or merchants were vital. This gave them some advantage within society, and authority could be exemplified through a direct leadership role, governing behind the scenes, or from a domestic perspective within the hearth.

5. The Amazons of Dahomey.

The different roles that men and women played in pre-colonial African societies were often demarcated. Typically, women were involved in processing food, managing the home, caring for children and the elderly, and marketing and selling surplus products. The males classically gathered the harvest, hunted for food, and defended the community with arms (although the female warriors of Dahomey demonstrated a variation in these norms) (Figure 5). Certainly, roles were assigned by sex, but gender roles were complementary and such balancing was vital for the society to prosper. In broad terms, women had identifiable roles within the community and, *generally*, women held a complementary, rather than subordinate position to men.

This is not to idealize pre-colonial Africa, however; there were indeed communities where social structures existed that prohibited women from realizing their full capacity. Many Islamic societies fell into this category, and as Islam spread across west Africa, its mores transformed previously fluid relations into rigid duties and obligations. The custom of secluding women from society spread with Islam, and the public role of females became limited. New social principles regarding what an ideal Muslim woman should be were developed. For example, in northern Nigeria, women had had a long history in textile manufacturing, but when the Sokoto Caliphate was established in 1809, Islamic law barred women from training as tailors, weavers, and garment embroiderers. Women were henceforth only allowed to spin, which limited their earning ability. In addition, in some societies, traditional succession to the throne or chieftainship had been matrilineal; after Islam arrived patrilinealism became dominant. Moreover, while Islam highly valued education, this was only for boys. Elsewhere, marital systems acted in ways to promote patriarchy. Traditional practices such as contract marriages to cement inter-communal ties, levirate marriages (where the brother of a deceased man is obliged to marry his brother's widow), widow inheritance, forced child marriages, polygamy, and dowries all put women at a disadvantage.

Nonetheless, pre-colonial African gender relations were, in general, complementary.

The effects of colonialism

Gender roles, like almost all other societal structures, were affected by European colonialism. Although varied in its effect, overall colonialism had a damaging influence on gender relations in Africa, altering the position of women in society and their capacity to play a part in it that both empowered them and which commanded respect. The cause of this was primarily through the imposition of patriarchal values and the economic system that colonialism brought to Africa. Colonialism appeared in Africa at precisely the time when, back in Europe, rigid gender roles were in existence. The norm of male-headed households where the man went out to work while the wife stayed at home, being utterly financially and socially dependent, was seen as natural and proper. The colonial authorities could thus not understand (or respect) different social structures when they were encountered in Africa. Equally, the sort of economic system that had reached its apogee in the mid-19th century, one where private property was sacred, class differences were acute, and people (i.e. males) needed to work to earn money to survive was dominant. Typical communal values that had existed before this system had been discarded in Europe, in some cases violently. What replaced them was an individualistic and misogynistic society, something that stood in contrast to most African ethics.

Indeed, it must be remembered that Africa was formally colonized at the height of European patriarchy. Women's economic and legal status in Europe had declined with the rise of capitalism and industrialization. The home was the marital unit where a married woman did not possess a separate legal identity under common law. In the ideal middle-class Victorian home, women and children (both idealized and infantilized at the same time) were constricted to the private household domain and were entirely dependent on the male head of the household. Women could not own property; they themselves *were* property. When this model was transported to the colonies, indigenous women's roles and privileges were discounted. The colonial system privileged men, disregarding indigenous gendered patterns in land usage, harvesting, types of compensation, and female knowledge. Across the continent, female farming systems were overturned and men were provided with the education, equipment, and incentives to engage in the newly introduced cash crops. The colonial legal systems equally privileged men and allowed them to sell land, eject women, and thrust them onto less productive pieces of land. The relegated economic status that women experienced was translated into politics, leading to women being pushed further from decision-making processes. What formalized education that was introduced (primarily by missionaries) favoured boys. In addition, colonialism established formal inequitable processes against women, including laws confining women to rural areas when men left for urban centres to work on the mines or engage in other wage labour. Colonial rule also gave the opportunity to local leaders and indigenous intermediaries to rationalize (and in some cases invent) 'tradition' in ways that favoured authoritative male figures and further sidelined women and the young. Thus, the values imposed by colonialism, in direct and indirect ways, structured gender inequality and female underdevelopment into African societies.

Post-colonial Africa

As noted previously, African societies differed greatly in how women contributed to societies and these differences were then changed, primarily for the worse, by the colonial experience. At independence, most new states granted women the franchise. However, societal norms often resulted in strong opposition to women playing particularly prominent roles in politics. Even during the independence struggles, women were often sidelined into women's wings of political parties. The practical effect was that these wings largely dealt with 'women's issues', while the 'real' core of politics was left in the hands of men. The type of patronage politics practised after independence, with its focus on the 'big men', has also contributed to the conviction that the political arena is not a place for women. Those women who do break through are often relatives of established politicians or (rarely) wealthy businessmen, and thus a class aspect to the marginalization of women emerges. Of course, both men and women have suffered due to the instability and disorder that has characterized a number of African states, all of which has exacerbated underdevelopment. This though has taken on a gendered dimension, in that women are generally at the bottom of the pile.

A key way in which women are prevented from taking on full roles in politics in Africa is through societal pressure. Men's assumed natural role as societal leaders is centred on the idea that they have authority over women. This entitlement of men often prohibits women from playing prominent roles in politics as it is assumed that political life is purely the territory of men. It is certainly true that African women are aware of, and often disapproving about, the nature of politics in Africa and the gendered way this is expressed. They may criticize cultural practices and patriarchal attitudes that perpetuate inequality (although generally hesitant to pass judgement on the often religious bases that may contribute to exclusion). However, while women may be critical of the patriarchal norms that reproduce women's exclusion from politics, they generally vacillate from contesting the status quo. This is because of their need to be seen as 'respectable' women within the societal understanding of what a woman's role is.

Indeed, within many societies, a woman's primary role is considered to be a 'respectable' wife and mother who cherishes family life and knows her place. A woman who takes part in politics is thus open to the charge that she is breaking societal conventions, operating outside the home, possibly away from her husband's supervision, in a milieu where she does not belong, and mixing with unrelated males in the public arena. Only prostitutes or women unwanted by men, due to various character faults, would do such a thing. Furthermore, given that many political meetings are organized in the evening after work hours, a woman who participates in such get-togethers must, it is believed, clearly be sleeping with the attending males or up to other nefarious activities. If married, an aspiring female politician has to gain the support of her husband. In the aforementioned societal context, a husband who agrees to a political role for his wife may very well be scorned for having lost control of his woman. Derision or the fear thereof may make it very problematic for a woman to obtain her husband's backing. This is difficult as a husband's support, beyond the requirements for financial largesse, is seen as an overriding precondition for female participation in politics. This support may, of course, be withdrawn at any time, which is usually devastating for a female politician's societal standing. The norms of respectability, motherhood, and domestic responsibility powerfully serve to dissuade many women from taking on political roles. Despite all this, women have in recent years begun mobilizing.

Political mobilization

One of the interesting features of contemporary African political life is that women's organizations have proliferated in recent years. On the continent, there is a wide divergence in terms of the nature and effectiveness of women's pressure groups. With the rise of new technologies, continental networking of activists has also developed, emboldening some women to push for greater equity. Such movements, which are focused on the status of women in society, are invariably a result of processes that may be re-defining gender roles. This does not mean that all organizations are progressive, however; some women's groups have been absorbed with a conservative agenda to defend traditional female family roles in the face of perceived disempowering trends such as urbanization and modernization. Such groups cannot be said to be feminist in the traditional sense of the word.

Organizations that can be considered feminist are groups that challenge patriarchal attitudes. These use a gendered analysis of society and question the political, economic, and social structures that underpin male domination and disempower women. Examples would include women's groups mobilized around sexual health or property rights. The HIV/AIDS pandemic in much of Africa, for instance, served as the midwife for a variety of women's organizations that at first focused on infection prevention strategies but moved on to wider gender issues within society. Elsewhere, African women have progressively expanded their roles in society by forming credit associations for small-scale women traders, and developed female farming associations to share farming techniques and agricultural knowledge as well as mutual assistance societies to develop support networks. By acting in this way, women have exercised a degree of autonomy, even if in substitute spaces different from conventional male-dominated society.

African women have also created coalition and advocacy networks to shape policies. These networks have permitted women to animate followers at the grassroots level all the way up to state policy level. Beyond that, an increasing presence internationally by African women activists demonstrates a wider trend. The Kenyan environmental political activist and Nobel Laureate Wangari Maathai is emblematic of such a development, but there are many more. The rise of the Internet has accelerated this process, instantly putting women from across the continent and beyond in contact with each other. The emancipatory power of information and communication technologies will no doubt continue to energize women's mobilization in Africa. Major challenges remain, not least the societal norms that in some countries block active female participation in formal politics. Equally, the economic status of women very much informs how they encounter patriarchal attitudes. Nonetheless, if politics is understood as beyond the official institutional expressions of parliaments and ministerial positions, women are already at the heart of politics in Africa.

Post-conflict societies

Finally, an interesting phenomenon in Africa is that countries that have experienced prolonged conflict tend to have higher rates of female political representation than countries that have not undergone violence. Post-conflict Liberia was the first African country to elect a female president (in 2006) while Uganda had a female vice-president in 1994. As noted, post-genocide Rwanda has the world's highest ratio of female parliamentary representation in the world, something it has maintained since 2003. Countries that have emerged out of serious political violence have been speedier in promoting women's rights and voting in females to political positions than less conflicted African states. Furthermore, such post-conflict countries have gone further in modifying laws and constitutions to provide greater gender equity and to deliver stronger legal securities with regard to familial law, land rights, and gendered violence. Africa is not unique in this regard, but it is a noteworthy trend.

Within such societies, outside of political life, women are generally more visible in commerce, civil society, academia, and other institutions. Changes in attitudes regarding women and their role in society seem to account for this phenomenon. During war, women are propelled into fresh responsibilities in society and the economy, often to take up the slack from the men who are directly involved in violence. At the same time, women have been at the forefront of peace movements demanding a cessation to conflict. They have then benefited from transitions to peace by pressing for greater equality. As most women were not involved in the violence, they possess a degree of trustworthiness that men do not; they may be seen as politically neutral and/or not tainted by the conflict and thus as a clean pair of hands.

Thus, during peace negotiations, a degree of political capital can be expended on incorporating gender issues into peace agreements, which then filters through into wider society and opens up greater space for female participation. Post-conflict states may very well have quotas for women candidates in elections, the proliferation of rape during the conflict may well have changed attitudes towards sexual violence, and, in general, women's issues are taken more seriously. Funding from the international community to support programmes associated with these matters may well help consolidate progress. Clearly, only a few countries have followed this path and it is certainly not a model that can or should be pursued. However, it is intriguing that societies that have experienced a rupture from the past—through either violence or revolution—tend to have new norms and institutions that may very well be conducive for greater gender equity moving forward.

Chapter 6
The role of identity in African politics

A common perception of African politics is that identity—principally *ethnic* politics—dominates and that this profoundly distorts governance, weakens the sense of national identity, promotes instability, and, in worst-case scenarios, leads to violence. However, like all other political phenomena in Africa, the reality of underdevelopment explains matters more clearly. Given its levels of development, Africa is no more divided by identity than other parts of the world. Notably, however, except where some form of industrialization took place (primarily in southern Africa), class has been weak as an organizing vehicle and other forms of social identity—primarily ethnic and religious—have been dominant.

It should be stated that in the study of Africa, ethnicity in particular has been controversial. This is primarily because of the colonial fixation with 'tribes', which were seen as reflecting a pre-modern way of life that privileged primordial ties. Colonial administrators made great efforts in classifying and delineating different groups in Africa, leading to the assertion that Africa was made up of thousands of 'tribes' speaking innumerable languages. Of course, they all hated each other and thus needed the Europeans to maintain peace. Thus one of the justifications of colonial rule was born. Even today, the word 'tribe' is often used in a negative sense, implying primitivism and backwardness. That nations such as Hausa (thirty-five million people), Fulani (twenty-seven million), and Zulu (eleven million) are still labelled as 'tribes' by some, while the Danes (five million), Welsh (2.6 million) and Manx (80,000 people) never have this label thrust upon them, is indicative of this mentality.

It is true that in societies where class-consciousness is weak, other identities such as religion, nationality, ethnicity, etc. usually arise and may be the organizing principle around which political mobilization may take place. Nevertheless, identity politics are symptoms of Africa's underdevelopment, not the cause, and the prominence of such political mobilization reflects much deeper structural problems facing many post-colonial states. With regards to ethnicity, it itself is something constructed and various communities now labelled ethnic groups came to be initiated during colonial rule, where a sense of togetherness developed, often in response to alien rule. Typically, ethnicities have been open-ended rather than static; groups have appeared and disappeared, changed their monikers, and fought over who is and who is not a genuine member of the community. However, although assuredly fabricated to a degree, identity is also unmistakably real and has developed a life of its own. Exacerbated by underdevelopment and other factors, identity politics attains real-life status.

Before the colonial era, as has been noted, various parts of Africa functioned as communities with state institutions in a particular location where territory and a particular identity broadly overlapped. The kingdoms of Dahomey (present-day Benin), Buganda (Uganda), and Rozwi (Zimbabwe) would be examples (Figure 6). Elsewhere, communities, where identities on occasion overlapped and there was linguistic and cultural borrowing alongside various types of governance between the different communities, existed. In the main, African societies were based on notions of identity, such as the family, ancestral lineage, the clan, or the community. Loose federations of these groups with cultural, religious, and linguistic features in common were the

6. Great Zimbabwe ruins.

pre-colonial units of socio-economic institutes and informed
relations with other neighbouring communities.

Colonial rule, which forced together different communities (some
of which were traditionally hostile to each other) was mainly
responsible for producing the situation found today where very
few nation states (in the sense that a relatively homogeneous people
inhabits a sovereign state) exist. The number of such states, namely
Lesotho, Somalia, and eSwatini, demonstrates just how profound
the impact of colonialism was on previous polities. In the rest of
Africa, most states are multicultural, with often a wide variety
of communities, be they ethnic, religious, or regional in nature,
living within a country's borders.

Colonial rule

Colonial powers invariably sought to lessen costs administering
their territories, thus amalgamating communities together into
colonial units was the norm. These administrative economies
of scale and the minimization of bureaucratic costs led to the

manufacturing of large colonial states, which incorporated multiple communities. For example, *Afrique équatoriale française*, with its capital in Brazzaville, comprised what are today the countries of Chad, the Central African Republic, Cameroon, the Republic of the Congo, and Gabon. *Afrique occidentale française*, with its capital in Dakar, was made up of what are today Mauritania, Senegal, Mali, Guinea, Côte d'Ivoire, Burkina Faso, Benin, and Niger. In such circumstances, colonial rule often had to construct strategies to disguise the actual weakness of imperial regimes. Very few colonial territories had substantial numbers of either troops or administrators from the metropoles; the average British district commissioner was in charge of a territory the size of Wales. Thus, forging alliances with traditional elites, known as 'indirect rule', was practised, particularly by the British.

By relying on indigenous structures (and in some cases creating new ones), power relations at the local level were however altered and distinctions between communities exacerbated. When political control through proxies was practised, this elevated some above others, both individually or collectively. This system was based on purportedly homogenous rural 'tribal' areas, each with their own 'tribal' leaders who acted as decentralized despots on behalf of colonialism. The policy led in some territories to the invention of new 'tribes' as the colonialists broke up African communities into separate areas, each with their own chiefs, encouraging division and difference. Here it should be noted that African societies were not simply passive in this process and actors within these communities were active participants, raising their status.

In addition, colonial rule controlled both migration between different areas and property rights, restricting them to the 'natives' of the localized area. This further encouraged fractionalization among African populations. The imposition of colonial frontiers also served to affect inter-communal relations. Obviously, at the time when borders were being drawn up in Berlin, the local situation on the ground was largely irrelevant to the consideration of pencil lines on maps drawn by Europeans.

Utilizing classic divide and rule tactics, indigenous social structures within British Africa were retained. However, it was often the case that the colonialists would privilege people from the lesser communities, who often had complaints against the more dominant groups. These would then be provided with Western education and then appointed to positions in the colonial civil service or police force. This exploitation (and, in some cases, creation) of communal differences served to inhibit pan-ethnic organization against colonialism. Elsewhere, religion was used; in Nigeria, colonial rule meshed religion and ethnicity to become the preeminent markers of identity even today. The practical effect of indirect rule was that it divided African peoples into artificially engineered classifications of difference that have often lasted long after the colonialists have left. Imbalance under colonialism thus strengthened antagonisms between communities. In Nigeria for example, the Christian South attained a greater level of social development than the Muslim North, while in Uganda the Protestant Baganda moved ahead of all other groups. The Asante, Bemba, and Kikuyu were similarly privileged relative to other communities in Ghana, Zambia, and Kenya, respectively. Since Kenyan independence, inter-communal relationships have in fact been typified by the hostility of all Kenyan groups to the Kikuyu. In the French colonies, Paris centralized the colonial governments and sought to assimilate compliant inhabitants into the French language and culture. This created a new elite group of Gallicized administrators who often felt superior to the 'natives' who retained their communal attachments. Decades after independence, Francophone Africa is replete with elite Africans who think of themselves as Black Frenchmen and -women, and look to Paris for guidance and support.

In addition, colonization was based on domination and lacked legitimacy. As defence mechanisms against this alien rule, Africans often resorted to traditional identities for solidarity; ethnicity was one of these, alongside religion. These self-groupings provided camaraderie, a sense of self-worth, and in turn emerged as sites of resistance against colonialism. However, they also divided the African public space along identity lines. As urbanization grew in many African territories, migrants from the rural areas often gravitated towards these associations, further solidifying the ethnic or religious aspects of political organization among the colonized. Leaders who emerged from these groups naturally drew support on the basis of how their organizations were formed.

Overall, it can be said that colonial authorities concretized differences among and between the subjugated. While Europeans and other immigrants (such as Indians or Lebanese) were subject to civil law, indigenous people were subject to customary law, which was peculiar to each community. Africans thus became tribal natives within a governance system that encompassed them within an assortment of mutually exclusive categories, each with its own discrete customs and domains. At the localized level, indigenous elites deployed their newly strengthened power emanating from colonial authority to police their own communities. Not only did this head off any local mobilization against colonialism (which in practical terms would challenge the local chiefs' positions) but it also allowed the development of an exaggerated top–down form of governance that disempowered ordinary people.

The de-colonization period further contributed to the politicization of identity. Numerous nationalist movements had their origins in identity groups, mostly ethnic- or religious-based. As long as the different groups had a common enemy (i.e. the colonialists), cooperation was desired. However, such collaboration began to break down on the eve of independence as the different leaders contrived to take power. In a wider milieu where class identity was largely undeveloped, those political leaders who came from the larger communities often utilized identity politics to strengthen their political support. This was where tribalism (the illegitimate exploitation of ethnic identities for political purposes) and sectarianism came to the fore. As independence approached, the focus of political activity swung from anti-colonialism to schemes for gaining as much as possible. Communities who felt that they would be disadvantaged or in perpetual minority status once the Europeans left started to feel concerned about being sidelined or dominated by others, in some cases their traditional nemeses. A sudden increase of civic organizations based on identities, all demanding guarantees and taking the form of parties seeking federalism, minority rights, autonomy, or even outright separatism, transpired. Anxieties over domination by 'The Other', this time the different local rather than the European, became intrinsic to many African countries moving towards freedom.

A good example of this trend may be found in Nigeria, where the main administrative divisions were constructed by the British to match the geographic whereabouts of the three chief ethnicities. When nationalist organizations began to press for greater self-rule, London devolved authority to these areas, granting self-government under the control of regional premiers. The three principal nationalist kingpins, Nnamdi Azikiwe in the east, Obafemi Awolowo in the west, and Alhaji Ahmadu Bello in the north, elected to locate their power in their home regions rather than continuing in the British-controlled central government. Nigeria thus rapidly became dominated by the three regionally based parties, which themselves drew on ethic identities for support. At independence, Nigeria was thus born already riven with contesting loyalties and strong regional characteristics that did nothing to promote national unity or a politics that was able to transcend ethnic and religious divisions. The Biafran War (1967–70) was a result of mutual suspicion and antagonisms organized along religious and ethnic lines and centred around access to material wealth (e.g. oil).

Elsewhere, such as in Rwanda and Burundi, the colonialists explicitly favoured one group over another, leading to huge disparities in terms of education levels and general well-being between the dominant Tutsis and the disadvantaged Hutus (who constituted the majority of the population). Right on the eve of independence, the Belgian authorities switched sides and began boosting the Hutus. The result was political violence and an absolute entrenchment of ethnicity as being the marker of politics in those two countries. The genocide of 1994 was the result.

Post-independence Africa

The vast majority of African leaders who came to power after the Europeans departed simply assumed control of the colonial state, doing very little to transform its structures and logics. Initially, many African leaders sought to renounce identity politics, at least rhetorically. National unity was elevated: the national mottoes of most African countries thus stress unity: *Unité, Travail, Progrès* (Burundi), *Unidad, Paz, Justicia* (Equatorial Guinea), and *One Zambia, One Nation* being examples. Elsewhere, such as in Ghana, it was made illegal to organize parties along ethnic lines while Julius Nyerere, himself the son of a chief, sought to eradicate disunity by promoting a strong sense of Tanzanian nationalism.

However, other leaders sought to utilize identity for their own profit. Jomo Kenyatta of Kenya became a master of ethnic intrigue, crafting alliances of different ethnic groups under the supremacy of the Kenyan African National Union. His successor, Danial arap Moi, took this manipulation to a different level upon succession, leaving Kenya today chronically divided along ethnic lines. In Côte d'Ivoire, Félix Houphouët-Boigny brought on board different ethnic communities through the astute allocation of government positions, making sure that all notable groups felt they had a share in the country. The management of patronage indeed became a significant way in which many post-colonial leaders dealt with problems associated with ethnicity, religion, or regionalism. While there were sufficient resources to lubricate the system, such manipulations worked to a degree. Yet once the economies of many African states went into serious decline from the mid-1970s onwards, the ability to nourish such systems rapidly diminished. As opposition mounted, the centralization of power, increasingly oppressive management techniques, and the denial of basic rights became normal. Many leaders succumbed to the notion that only *their* community could be trusted and, in turn, this generated reactions from wider society who felt excluded. This was often expressed through intensifying tensions between communities.

Indeed, as the independence dream began to fade and the new countries had to face underdevelopment, inequality, and the machinations of external forces, the post-colonial state became increasingly repressive and centred around a small clique of political actors. This centralization of power along autocratic lines served to stress identity politics as people turned to solidarity groups in response. This was particularly the case if some groups sought to impose their languages and religion on others. If the state was seen to have been 'captured' by representatives of a particular group, non-members of that group tended to identify the state as being illegitimate and serving only the interests of a particular ethnicity, region, or religion. Identity thus became further politicized. Political mobilization then increasingly took on the form of effective competition between different groups. This politics was not based on any meaningful political programmes, but merely on which party represented which group. Patron–client systems that came to dominate politics in many African countries similarly became organized around identity to establish and maintain support networks.

The result was the introduction of struggles and competing factions based on exclusivity grounded in membership of a particular identity group. In the vast majority of cases, this identity group was founded in ethnicity and/or religion. In such situations, identity has become very real and ideologies have emerged from inter-group hostilities. Non-members became putative rivals, even if their social status was identical. Religion and ethnicity then became a useful resource for manipulation by politicians and other entrepreneurs. Just as the colonialists had practised divisive tactics, many post-colonial leaders utilize identities as a means to an end: re-directing popular disillusionment away from them to The Other.

Democratization and identity

From the late 1980s onwards, Africa saw a generalized movement towards liberal democracy. Under pressure from both domestic constituencies and external actors, many African states went through the process of formal elections. While promising a change in the manner of governance, what transpired in various countries was the continued manipulation of identity for political mileage. Rather than fashion cross-community political parties based on political principles and actual policies, when many African states moved from one party rule to multiparty democracy, identity configurations developed along party lines. Indeed, multiparty democracy has seen a continuation of malgovernance, corruption, and patronage politics, while chauvinism has been encouraged by some political leaders. For instance, in Kenya, ethnicized politics and often violence has been witnessed in all the elections held since 1991 when Kenya embraced multiparty democracy, while in the Central African Republic, politicians have manipulated identities to pit Christians against Muslims. Effectively, while countries remained single-party states, identity could be more easily managed, if not suppressed. Competitive politics in some countries, however, set loose all the political dynamisms previously kept at bay.

Crucially, democratization often occurred side by side with neo-liberal structural adjustment programmes (SAPs) promoted by the West. These reform projects ushered in an unprecedented increase in economic inequalities, significant declines in life expectancy, and an extraordinary growth in the share of Africans living in absolute poverty. This was also associated with deterioration in the rural sectors and huge population flows to the urban areas. Cuts in the number of civil servants and social services as part of the SAPs served to hollow out many states, diminishing their capacity to operate and shrinking the effective power of already weak states to a limited area around the capital and major towns. De-regulation and liberalization broadened the politicization of key segments of the national economy as they shifted from state control to private hands, and many incumbent elites became rich through corruptly managing this process. Where they came from specific groups, non-members tended to read this as an illegitimate communal takeover of the national wealth. At the same time, the deterioration of the state and the subsequent competition for control of resources in a situation where poverty and inequality were growing increased both the horizontal and the vertical inequalities between and within different communities. For instance, the decline in state capacity and control over resources as privatization proceeded meant that there was a reduction in the resources available to political actors to service their patronage networks and to alleviate the growing inequalities between different groups. In addition, the weakening of state capacity resulted in a situation by the late 1980s where governance was in crisis and the state was seen as unable to solve the mounting problems. Political entrepreneurs stepped into the breach, promising that they would defend and advance the interest of specific communities through mobilization around identity politics. The result was a further fracturing of society.

The experience in Africa showed that transitions to democracy can be fraught with uncertainty, and under conditions of inequality and underdevelopment this may fuel ethnic and religious fervours. The problem is the way in which underdevelopment and inequity combine with the insecurities felt by members of society undergoing transitions. Communal competition may emerge re-invigorated from such a milieu, shaping a great deal of the actual transitions to democracy and then the subsequent practices of how these ostensibly liberal democracies operate. At a most basic level, the struggle to survive under conditions of relative scarcity can, when the public space is opened for contestation, give birth to or intensify existing rivalries between communities. The more limited the available resources, the more likely that identity politics becomes problematic. If politics is about who gets what, when, and how, political mobilization along identity lines provides the answer: *us* and not *them*.

Concluding thoughts

Identity by itself is not problematic. It is possible—indeed usual—to prefer to associate with like-minded people, and this does not mean that one is antagonistic to other groups. The problem of identity politics in Africa is the way its more negative manifestations, primarily tribalism and sectarianism, are exploited by actors for material gains and political support. Problems arising from the appeal to identity to hide exploitation by the rich and prevent solidarity along class lines occur throughout the world and are by no means unique to Africa. A complicating factor in the African situation, however, is the weakness of reliable institutions to control and minimize antagonistic politics along identity lines and the legacy of colonization, which very much entrenched a rather static vision of 'tribes', which became easily manipulated by predatory elites.

However, it is important to note that some of the pathologies noted previously are not predicaments restricted to religion or ethnicity; they are problems associated with particular political dynamics in Africa, which materializes around identity issues. To repeat, they are symptoms, not causes, of the malaise that grips some African countries: *identity per se is not the cause of Africa's problems*. Rather, it is the lack of meaningful development and the way in which labels and identification have been exploited which is the problem. Conflicts (including the Rwandan genocide) have been responses to failed development projects and the subsequent inequalities that this has engendered. Identity in these cases comes to be held up as the scapegoat for everything that has gone wrong. Consequently, solutions to such problems must tackle the political issues in question, not identity.

It is of course true that groups often have their own prejudices and stereotypes about each other, but these attitudes have not normally turned into conflict at the people-to-people level, unless manipulated and organized by political leaders. Elites find prejudices and stereotypes fertile ground in which they can cultivate support for their political and economic aspirations. Expressing their objectives in communal terms gives them more legitimacy, in the same way that nationalism has been used to beat the drums of war elsewhere. The major beneficiaries of such aspirations are the elites. Identity is clearly a tool used by people for various reasons (political, social, economic, and so on) rather than something that comes from within 'naturally', and Africa is no different from anywhere else in the world in this regard. The key issue though is the nature of post-colonial African politics (based on patronage) and relative scarcity. This means that the question of control (and sharing or distribution) of state power and resources exacerbates societal tensions and this can be mobilized along communal lines at times. Economic marginalization provides a much stronger guide than identity to the incidence of societal conflict. As Alexis de Tocqueville wrote, 'Remove the secondary causes that have produced the great convulsions of the world and you will almost always find the principle of inequality at the bottom'.

Chapter 7
The military in African politics

A coup d'état is an extra-constitutional or forced change of government, literally a 'strike against the state'. Africa has been one of the continents worst affected by coups and other interventions by the armed forces into politics: since the 1960s there have been more than 200 coups in Africa, with around half of them being successful. Very few countries have enjoyed uninterrupted democracy since independence, and prior to the 1990s, military coups were 'normal' in many countries. Indeed, between 1960 and 1982, almost 90 per cent of independent African states had been subjected to a coup, an attempted coup, or a plot. The trend began very early on in the post-colonial era, with the first coup taking place in Togo, less than three years after independence. The 1960s to the 1990s saw an average of around twenty successful coups per decade across Africa, a period that was characterized by Cold War machinations, economic crises, and the growing de-legitimization of many post-colonial regimes. During this era, very few leaders left power after losing elections. Some did retire voluntarily (Aden Abdullah Osman in Somalia in 1967; Léopold Senghor in Senegal in 1980; Ahmadou Ahidjo in Cameroon in 1982; and Julius Nyerere in Tanzania in 1985) but most of those did so after handpicking their own successor. Elsewhere, being the head of state of an African country was a decidedly risky occupation. Of the different sub-regions in Africa, west Africa experienced the greatest number of coups (both successful and failed) while central and east Africa followed, with southern Africa having had the smallest number.

The majority of coups were followed by the formation of some type of military government, but after this diverse outcomes resulted. After all, the military is not monolithic and various factions within it may lead a coup. Typically, senior military officers have often associated themselves with the political class in power and have significant self-interest in maintaining the status quo. Younger officers have inclined to identify with their own generation among the political elites and the bureaucracy; if that generation itself is unfavourable to the extant political order, its sympathetic cohorts in the military may deploy to re-order the system. However, the key coup-making rank tends to be those at the rank of colonel and other middle grades. These have command of a substantial number of soldiers and also possess access to military communications and weapons supplies. The end result of any such intervention varies. In some cases, rivals toppled the initial coup leaders; in others, the military went back to their barracks, although the threat of another intervention was never far away. Elsewhere, and this became a tendency from the 1990s onwards, those who assumed power through a coup 'civilianized' their status, taking off their uniforms and holding elections (of varying authenticity) to legitimize their status as heads of state (Figure 7).

In all cases, the political culture of a country that experiences a military intercession is irrevocably altered. Indeed, a notable characteristic of military coups is that with almost every coup there is a subsequent counter-coup or linked plotting and intrigue; coups tend to engender other coups. Reasons, consequences, and the principle on which the coup was ostensibly launched may vary, but once the military genie is out of the bottle, it is very difficult to put it back in. Indeed, once the military violates a key tenet of their role in society—that armies are subordinate to the state—the original intervention sets off a chain reaction. A good example in

7. Aftermath of a coup, Cotonou, 1965.

this regard is Benin. Independent in 1960, in 1963 the government was deposed in a coup led by the army's chief of staff. Although a civilian was elected president a year later, in 1965 the military again assumed power. Two years later a rival faction within the army took power, only to see their nominated president overthrown in 1969. Presidential elections held in 1970 were abandoned and in 1972 a middle-ranking officer seized power, only handing over to civilian rule again in 1991.

In thinking about coups in Africa, the motives which inspire the military to do what they do may be broken down into various factors. Some seem to have been provoked by widespread societal dissatisfaction with the nature and policies of the political class in power. These coups often enjoy broad popular support (at least initially) and are justified as being necessary to 'drain the swamp' of incompetent and corrupt politicians. Upon assuming power, coup leaders typically make media commitments to respect civil liberties, promote economic development, and lay a solid foundation for return to democracy. Such pledges often initially sway public opinion, especially the illiterate and uneducated, who view the military as a messiah. Capturing radio and TV stations is usually a first priority for coup leaders so that they can indeed reassure the public.

However, launched to allegedly improve public order, efficiency, or to end corruption, there is usually no fundamental shift in the structure of power: such coups take on the form of mere musical chairs at the highest levels of society. As a result, they may be repeated again and again. Somewhat linked to these types of coups are those interventions which are embarked on to supplant a government deemed to be unable or unwilling to preserve the state from internal or external problems. Again, these may be at first popular. Other types are less able to enjoy support. Coups which are motivated mostly by the ambitions of individuals who utilize the military to capture power and its subsequent rewards are clearly of self-interest, as are interventions which are driven by actual or imagined complaints from the military institutions against the regime in power (often around pay and privileges). Perhaps most destructive are those interventions where the army makes a move to prevent mass participation and social mobilization. These tend to be the worst kind because many civilians may be killed. However, identifying the real motives behind the coup plotters is extremely difficult given that all of them justify their actions with reference to the 'national interest'. Often only a retrospective analysis may help explain what led to the intervention. In any event, it is also likely that the motives and the intentions, or what the coup leaders hope to achieve, change over time, in some cases quite rapidly.

Yet a division can be made between those coups that clearly serve the interests of the political establishment and those that may act as catalysts for substantial breaks from the past. This distinction certainly held much more water during the first three decades of independence when revolutionary coups heralded some quite dramatic societal transformations. The overthrow of Haile Selassie

in Ethiopia in 1974 is perhaps the most emblematic, alongside
Thomas Sankara's 1983 coup in Upper Volta (now Burkina Faso).
In these and other cases, the military seized power and then
proceeded to institutionalize a political and economic programme
of reform, of varying success and longevity. However, at least these
interventions had some sort of project. The majority of coups
across Africa have, in contrast, been characterized by subsequent
inertia, the reproduction of existing problems within society,
and have often been accompanied by a further closing down
of political space.

Nature of military rule

By definition, a military regime is built on force and coercion,
rather than consent. Militaries are not democracies but deeply
hierarchical institutions characterized by essentially dictatorial
norms. By their very modus operandi, they are incompatible with
constitutional democracy. As a result, when militaries seize power,
two dominant factors tend to shape their time in power. The first
is the need (expressed or otherwise) to dominate civil society.
Alternative voices or possible sites of opposition (interpreted
through the military prism as unconscionable insubordination)
cannot be allowed. Second, the desire to secure the military's
power base engenders a strong dictatorial attitude. Although often
welcomed by the civilian population, disillusion with military rule
generally quickly sets in, and to remain in control the military
must resort to naked force. The levels of this may vary, but the
message that needs to be sent out to the ill-disciplined civilian
population is that the army is in charge. Consequently, military
regimes tend to have a disturbing contempt for the law and
quickly degenerate into simply staying in power, perceiving
themselves to be above legal constraints. In such circumstances,
there is little accountability or respect for citizens' rights, as
ultimate authority on the legality of government action lies not
with the courts, but with the military. In any case, laws, processes,
and institutions of rights are typically abrogated or severely

restricted, often under 'states of emergency'. Typical events surrounding coups include the constitution being suspended, political parties being disbanded, and civil liberties being severely circumscribed. All of these herald the military's desire to neutralize constraints on their exercise of state power.

The military accomplishes this in various ways. The first is to assign itself legislative and executive powers greater than the normal legal processes. This is achieved through the military insulating itself from judicial review, often through the wholesale dismissal of the judiciary and the suspension of the functioning of courts. Another, alluded to previously, is the abridgement of civil liberties. As emergency powers have been instituted, this is relatively easy to do and there is no recourse for affected individuals. Finally, the military often assigns itself adjudicator functions, utilizing tribunals staffed by military or compliant members of the judiciary. Military courts thus replace civilian magistrates, with predictable results.

In many African countries, politics often revolves around personalities rather than ideology. In such circumstances, things tend to get personal very quickly. One feature of military rule is that the coup leaders often use the opportunity afforded to them by the seizure of power to settle old scores, silence enemies from the previous regime, and get revenge. In such situations, coups may be quite bloody, as payback for actual or perceived slights to the dignity of the military can be expressed through violence. Equally, eliminating potential rivals from both within and without the military is an understandable rational action by coup leaders. After all, if a precedent is set that involves the military overthrow of a civilian government, there is no moral barrier to other elements using the same tactics to replace the new incumbents.

Overall, military rule tends to severely damage the polity. Citizens who do not submit to or align themselves with the military are shut out from the nation's economic and social activities and the political class may become defunct. On the other hand, loyalty and support for the military can significantly enhance one's career and generate considerable wealth; there are numerous examples whereby figures associated with coups have enriched themselves. The worst example to date is probably Sani Abacha, who led a military coup and then controlled Nigeria from 1993 to 1998. Up to $4 billion in foreign assets were traced to Abacha, his family, and their representatives after he died. Other military rulers have been perhaps less ambitious, but looting the state has been a feature of most army regimes, notwithstanding the fact that upon assuming power, reining in corruption and promoting good governance was ostensibly the main reason why the military intervened.

Why so many coups?

In all cases, the involvement of the military in the political realm is a symptom of a wider structural malaise within the post-colonial state. The fragility of the state and its tenuous hold on legitimacy, accentuated by the behaviour of those in power, is of critical importance. At the time of independence, no indigenous business class existed that had the scope and depth to assume power. Rather, the state was handed over to a set of leaders who rapidly embarked upon transforming political governance into personal wealth. The demonstrable accomplishments of these politicians in enriching themselves and their families and cliques fuelled jealousy and competition. Given that in many countries the opportunities to change the political class through the ballot box were constrained or non-existent, the only agents able to effect change became the military. In conditions of protracted economic crisis and the failure of political leadership, inter-elite squabbling and lingering political crises may lead to disappointment and loss of faith in civilian government. Measures to address the economic crisis (such as price controls, currency restrictions, increased taxes, devaluation, etc.) are generally unpopular and so the civilian regimes appear paralysed. In these circumstances, the arrival of the military momentarily throws up the possibility of change.

Factors internal to the military itself may also play a role. Much of the military leadership in Africa have been sent abroad for training and often see themselves as superior, better educated, and more professional than the political class. Replacing the bumbling amateurs with their self-perceived discipline and know-how may tempt some officers. The military establishment is a strong force in politics in many African countries, and its leaders may perceive themselves as being able to 'cleanse the nation' of corrupt politicians. In such cases, a form of 'Bonapartism' takes place whereby there is a belief that a strong state, based on and around a strongman or -woman, is required. The military usually supplies such candidates. Praetorianism (i.e. the control of a society by force) is then seen as the 'solution' to all the country's problems.

If the officer class does seize power, it can usually rely upon the compliance of the junior ranks, given that the non-commissioned ranks are often made up of peasant recruits, badly educated and on occasion exhibiting poor discipline. The 'typical' African army is often severely underpaid and may be unfamiliar with professional codes that prescribe non-interference with civilian matters. Membership of the military gives soldiers status and power, something that, of course, hugely increases when the army seizes control. Lording it over the civilian populace then provides all sorts of opportunities for the rank and file, and it is a fact that soldiers have been known to be wealth-seekers, property grabbers, and bribe-takers, openly engaging in self-enrichment activities over the barrel of a gun and through intimidation.

The 'ethnic/religious factor' may also play a role. Across Africa, societal tension and turmoil is often expressed through identity politics. One aspect of the colonial legacy that prepared the ground for some coups was the fact that the imperialists often recruited and promoted members of the military according to their ethnic origins, rather than merit. In Nigeria the Hausas were favoured, while in Uganda, northerners were seen as more 'martial' than the rest of the population. This meant that at independence,

African Politics

the military was dominated by one or two groups with shared origins who often assumed a bunker mentality versus the rest of the population. The results were predictable.

As mentioned, the personal ambitions and the craving for power by some key military players have also served to propel coups. There have been examples where officers have led coups to regain lost prestige or to preempt an impending purge. Indeed, inter-personal clashes have occurred between the civilian and military elites, and provoked takeovers, with some examples being Uganda in 1971, Congo-Kinshasa (then called the Republic of Congo; now, the DRC) in 1968, and Dahomey (now Benin) in 1967. The move by the military in Zimbabwe in late 2017 to replace Robert Mugabe and forestall the possibility of his wife assuming power was clearly motivated by personal ambitions and the desire to stave off the inevitable 'house cleaning' should Grace Mugabe become head of state.

While the various broad factors are widespread across the continent, not all countries experience regular coups and some never have. There is no hard and fast set of circumstances that enable any serious forecasting of where the next coup may take place. Indeed, the probability of a coup taking place seems to be independent of any topography (e.g. population size, land mass, natural resource endowments, social and economic development, ethnic diversity, and such like). Likewise, the kinds of governments in office, the types of bureaucracies, or the promotion of specific policies for economic development vary, as do the status and role of the military in countries' histories. At best, we may note a few tentative factors that seem to indicate the vulnerability of a country to a coup.

The first, and arguably most important, is the nature of the political culture of a given country. This often centres around the level of legitimacy that was established and then preserved by the formative political class. In some countries this has never existed in any meaningful sense. However, in others a national project of development and the construction of a capable state, with clearly delineated power positions, has meant that a military coup is mostly unthinkable and would be unlikely to receive any popular support. In yet other states the political class has held onto power tenuously and often blatantly corruptly, and no discernible benefits have accrued to the populace. In such circumstances, particularly when democratic space is shut off, the military option appears attractive. In other words, where civil society and institutions are weak and politics are corrupt and divisive, the military may carry the day if given an opportunity. The moment of opportunity often depends on finding a charismatic military leader and tapping into popular support. However, this is no hard and fast rule. For instance, until the coup in 1994, The Gambia had been perceived as one of the most stable countries in Africa, with an unbroken democratic record. Conversely, countries with acutely corrupt and autocratic regimes, such as Cameroon, Angola, and Eritrea, have avoided the fate of most of the continent (although attempts, of varying significance, have been made).

Decline in coups

Immediately after the end of the Cold War, it seemed that the frequency of coups in Africa was declining, and between 2000 and 2003 there were no coups at all. Although there have been a few instances since then, the overall incidence of coups is much lower now than in previous decades, as indicated in Table 5.

One important factor in reducing the likelihood of coups, one related to political culture, is the nature of governance reform that has taken place in many African countries. Coups *have* continued, but in comparison to previous eras, they have declined since the onset of multiparty politics. While not an entirely foolproof criterion, it appears that democracies that enjoy relative levels of legitimacy are less susceptible to military interventions. Although

Table 5. Incidence of coups in Africa, 1959–2018

Period	Successful coups d'état	Attempted/plotted coups d'état
1959–69	22	29
1970–9	20	35
1980–9	20	63
1990–9	16	60
2000–9	4	27
2010–18	6	21

in many countries the democratic process is fragile and incomplete, there is a growing agreement that institutionalized changes of government through the ballot box should be the only way in which a regime can be legitimately replaced. Thus any other measures to gain power are more and more unacceptable to the populace. A culture of the rule of law, constitutionalism, and democracy has increasingly undermined coup tendencies. Although coups have obviously not entirely disappeared from the African scene, the continent has witnessed progress in this regard.

In addition, the political culture at the continental level has changed with the creation of the African Union (AU). The haste with which both regional and pan-continental organizations now censure and suspend from membership states that have experienced coups has sent a clear and strong message that unconstitutional changes of government are no longer accepted without demur (as during the OAU period) and that membership of regional and continental bodies indicates acceptance of some basic norms. Previously, military leaders may have seized and then clung onto power with little or no criticism from their peers, as the OAU's observance of the principle of non-interference meant that there was a distinct lack of enthusiasm to take practical punitive steps if and when coups transpired. This has changed and now groups such as the Economic Community of West African States (ECOWAS), East African Community (EAC), Southern African Development Community (SADC), and the African Union (AU) actively contest such events. For instance, the AU's Constitutive Act includes pronounced principles on the advancement of democracy and good governance and prohibits coups. As a result, the effects of isolation through travel bans, sanctions, and suspension of membership of institutions now impose a cost on coup leaders hitherto not present.

Closing remarks

Beyond the immediate trigger causes of coups, which, as pointed out, may be multiple and unpredictable, two sets of causes may be identified that leads to a coup in Africa. Both are deep-seated and relate to the nature of the political economy of the continent. All African countries are profoundly dependent on external forces beyond their control, specifically in terms of their economies, which are almost completely dependent upon external demand. Thus, the economic controls at the disposal of political leaders are constrained. This means that the resolution of prolonged economic crises is often beyond the scope of those in control of the state; commodity prices rise and fall independent of any policy that may or may not be adopted. Whether governance is functional or dysfunctional, the position of a particular commodity in the global market may be the decisive factor that lies at the heart of the interminable state of underdevelopment and concomitant distorted political cultures. The second structural factor can be located in the pressures facing the post-colonial African state, which are typically expressed through high levels of personalism, patronage politics, and corruption.

Overall, prolonged military rule in the continent has further weakened the African state and served to delegitimize existing institutions, introducing even greater uncertainty into the political process. Where one or other identity group has dominated the military, coups have also helped further fracture society along religious and cultural lines. By its very nature, military governance impoverishes an already weak civil society and transposes the authoritarian values of military into civilian life. This contributes to the destruction of what 'normal' politics may have existed prior to the intervention. A political culture oriented towards the imposition of a command and control structure on the political process is entrenched and may be difficult to deconstruct. Finally, and perhaps just as serious as all the other legacies, is that coups leave a vestige of uncertainty and fear within the African polity. With the military having broken the taboo of interference in politics, the question that may remain in the minds of the political class (and indeed the general population) is when will the military next strike?

Chapter 8
Democracy in Africa

When discussing the issue of 'democracy' in Africa, it needs to be pointed out that most analyses focus on the formal procedures associated with Western liberal systems of rule. Certainly, the international community's attention is on elections and whether or not they can be evaluated as 'free and fair'. Other substantive issues around empowerment, development, and equity are invariably overlooked and a form of electoral fetishism dominates external involvement and interest in Africa's politics. Nevertheless, until the late 1980s, very few African countries experienced prolonged periods of electoral democracy. Indeed, only Botswana, The Gambia (until 1994), and Mauritius enjoyed such a status. Elsewhere, most countries were ruled by autocrats of varying stripes, ranging from presidents-for-life (as in Malawi's Hastings Banda) to more benign heads of state who, although not tyrannical, generally managed states without deeming it necessary to hold regular elections to test their popularity (or otherwise).

Modern Africa's first brush with formalized liberal democracy came in the form of various legislatures left behind by the leaving colonialists. Somewhat rudimentary facsimiles of their own types of government systems were bestowed on most Belgian, British, and French colonies (the Portuguese, a fascist dictatorship at the time their empire collapsed, left their colonies in chaos). Yet in the initial years of independence, most African leaders speedily enforced their own imprints on the states they had assumed control of, re-structuring or even abolishing the various institutions they controlled, often with reference to their unsuitability as colonial burdens inappropriate for African conditions. Ideas about specifically African forms of democracy were often used to justify what were essentially overbearing regimes. Leaders such as Kenneth Kaunda of Zambia, Kwame Nkrumah of Ghana, and Julius Nyerere of Tanzania argued that what was required was national unity and that multiparty democracy undermined this. One-party systems of government became the norm across Africa, and in the context of the Cold War, where regimes were supported with basically no questions asked, as long as the leader professed allegiance to the 'correct' side, dictatorships flourished.

The 'wave of democratization'

As superpower rivalry disappeared after the collapse of the Soviet Union in 1991, so too did the no-strings-attached support that had maintained many undemocratic African rulers for so long. Subsequently, the 1990s saw most of Africa experience a decline in single-party or no-party regimes and the introduction of multiparty systems. This was arguably the most momentous change in politics in Africa since the independence era. Various reasons accounted for this democratic wave in Africa. First, popular resentment against years of misrule had reached a tipping point. This, combined with the declining faculties of various ageing African leaders meant that change was in the air, something immeasurably boosted by the end of the Cold War and the resulting willingness of aid donors to put pressure on authoritarian regimes to change. The 'demonstration effect' in Eastern Europe, where longstanding regimes were overthrown, further emboldened opposition activists. These often linked up with a broad pool of political functionaries who had been left in the wilderness by extant regimes and who willingly put themselves forward as the faces of change. Increased conditioning of aid by donors and the pursuit of 'good governance' by the international community finally helped support transitions.

Subsequently, formal electoral democracy became far more common: between 1989 and 2000, thirty-five countries conducted more than one round of elections, and thirty-nine of the then forty-eight African legislative bodies comprised representatives from more than two separate political parties. The norms of presidential term limits and the requirement to hold free and fair elections were progressively introduced and, since that time, elections have become commonplace. However, the quality of Africa's democracies is uneven and expectations that the continent's political culture would be transformed by the institutionalization of regular elections have been disappointed in a number of countries. Problematically, the democracy advanced by donors in Africa refers to a system by which those elites that promise 'reform' and 'liberalization' and promote Western interests are supported. Popular involvement in decision-making is limited to periodic leadership choices via carefully managed elections. The promotion of such democracy has been instrumental in many cases in disempowering the majority by introducing the multiparty intonation as the panacea to Africa's problems, while entrenching ruling elites. As Jonathan Moyo put it:

> The assertion that the majority of African governments are now democratic is premised on contentious notions of democracy with external origins. Apart from this, the assertion has no empirical basis. It is true that multiparty elections are now common in Africa, but this truth does not describe a fundamental development. The change is strategic, not substantive.

In such formulations, the call to end corruption and mismanagement (a welcome call by any standards) and the push for democratic accountability (again, something which can be fully subscribed to) has become linked to a rather narrow understanding of democracy. Thus, while many African states have undergone 'democratization', such projects have largely been short-lived and/or contained what can only be regarded as a democratic façade. One need only think of the type of transitions that have occurred in states such as Malawi, Mozambique, and Zambia to acknowledge that there has been scant concrete progress for the average person.

Indeed, the very logic of personal rule and neo-patrimonial politics on the continent has meant that while there have been 'democratic transitions', there has been only a limited change in the political structures in most of Africa. Because political power grants one access to resources (customs revenues, foreign aid, possibly taxation, and, often, parastatals), elections on the continent are about much more than simply the chance to be the head of state and are almost life-and-death struggles for the ability to maintain oneself as a 'big man' (see Chapter 4). Political slogans for 'democracy' and an end to corruption are useful mobilizing devices and may even be believed by many ordinary people, but having captured political power, the new incumbent's clients will invariably anticipate and demand material benefits for their support. Thomas Callaghy notes that:

> Out of self-interest, many actors may support demands for democracy precisely because access to the state and to its resources will then become easier. Once democracy has been achieved, however, their behavior is not conducive to its consolidation. The characteristics of the patrimonial system reassert themselves.

Problematically, neither the voters nor the political competitors appear to be intrinsically opposed to such patronage systems if they perceive that benefits are coming in their direction. Rather, the aim is to be on the winning side, and even if the profits from such a system are unevenly circulated, those inside the loop and who gain from such arrangements do not complain—it is only when they slip out of the charmed circle that grievances and criticism against corruption generally emerge. The 'democratic transitions' of the late 1980s, rather than entrenching democracy on the continent, have instead amplified the pressure on political actors to disperse patronage.

Yet, even after political changes, the entrenchment of democratic values remains relatively shallow and compromised, even if such transitions have allowed a greater space to different voices to be heard these days, compared to the one-party era of the 1960s and 1970s. In general, African countries vary from reasonably open liberal democracies to barely disguised personal dictatorships. Some have established open and competitive democracies, such as Benin, Botswana, Ghana, Mauritius, Senegal, South Africa, etc. Others are countries where regimes with varying dictatorial leanings cling to power, often in the face of an increasingly emboldened opposition. Such countries would include Burundi, the Democratic Republic of Congo (DRC), Ethiopia, Uganda, Zimbabwe, etc. Elsewhere, repressive governments have managed to construct sufficient control over the political system that they have little to fear from holding 'elections'. Cameroon, Chad, and Rwanda are clear examples in this category. Finally, there are countries where outright domination is practised and where elections are either not held at all or are so farcical as to be of minimal value. Angola, Eritrea, and Equatorial Guinea fit into this category. The ratings assembled by Freedom House, an organization which gauges the levels of individual civil liberties, states that as of 2017, ten countries were ranked 'Free', nineteen 'Partly Free', and twenty 'Not Free'. In comparison, in 2009 the institution noted that nine countries were ranked 'Free', twenty-three 'Partly Free', and sixteen 'Not Free'. In other words, there appears to have been some backsliding in the consolidation of liberal democracy in Africa. But this is imbalanced and in fact geographically based: electoral democracy has noticeably grown in southern and west Africa, while east and central Africa have undergone a falling-off.

The varying outcomes experienced by African nations show that multiparty elections alone do not clearly signal a fundamental change in political culture, although there are indications that over time this may change. In spite of the fact that an electoral cycle can be organized with all the façade of a 'free and fair' process, its outward show may mask a variety of abuses that may constitute subterfuge by the incumbent elites to emerge with a renewed impression of legitimacy. Indeed, elections can result in a wide variety of regimes that are in essence anti-democratic, where transitions may be prevented by violence, where military oligarchies may emerge, and where new forms of autocracy may develop. Elections in such cases can be simply a method by which regime change can be coordinated among political and economic elites.

As has been noted previously, political rule in Africa is largely exemplified by patronage politics, often with ensconced big men maintained by patron–client networks that employ coercion and the manipulation of political processes to stay in power. In such circumstances, a form of zero-sum politics becomes dominant where those at the apex of power maintain a tight grip on material and coercive means to thwart rivals. Political success is realized through excluding (or incorporating) those deemed likely challengers. Under such circumstances, supremacy is retained through essentially corrupt methods and democratic values or considerations have little influence on the system. Although a form of accountability features as part of the patron–client structures, this largely functions as a guarantor of personal favours and benefits to a limited number of individuals, rather than as a mechanism to deliver public programmes aimed at broad-based development. The system is created to exploit state resources to create political alliances among and between social elites. Such leaders see access to the state as the main way to accumulate wealth and prestige. They are consequently vigilant in seeking to assert control and limit political spaces that get out of control and thus threaten their status. If elections really are required, such actors are very careful: as the former president of the Republic of Congo, Pascal Lissouba, once stated, 'one does not organize elections to end up on the losing side'.

Much of what has happened since the democratization wave of the early 1990s has confounded Western theorists of democracy. Elections were supposed to usher in a new way of doing things, with a public process of competition for power being facilitated by a free press, active civil society, and other standard indicators of openness. In fact, the euphoria in Africa about elections has tended to conceal a number of underlying problems that have not gone away completely. Chief among these is the lack of a political culture of compromise, but equally important is the fact that the major aim of many democracy movements has been to overthrow an existing government, rather than install a workable, free, and sustainable system of participatory politics. Certainly the language of democracy and liberty is used, but once a new cadre entrenches itself in power, business has continued. The trend has been that every time organized social movements manage to accomplish their goals, often after a struggle with the incumbents in power, rather than retain their structure, integrity, and autonomy, they either join up with the new regime, align with assorted interest groups (usually based on identity politics), or disband. This cycle is then repeated.

Despite the potential for multiparty elections to move Africa away from autocratic patron–client structures, many leaders have learnt how to utilize the system of elections as a tactic to grant their control increased legitimacy. Elections in various countries have in such cases been more symbolic than transformational, ending with results whereby leaders and their cliques retain their power without being subjected to any profound change in their behaviour. Domination of the legislative and judicial bodies, the media, and the exploitation of the state's resources have remained in their hands. In such cases, the only substantial difference between their governance in the context of electoral politics and the former outright autocratic system is that multiparty politics has to take place with at least the appearance of an opposition. But this is often weak and beset with factions and in any case can be often bought off with promises of wealth and privileges. In these circumstances, dominant political actors have kept their *de facto* absolute power while administering a *de jure* democratic state; the major change has been that their behaviour is now mitigated by an ostensibly more legitimate system that implies popular backing.

Such phenomena frequently occur where leadership change has not happened in over ten years. Examples here would include Cameroon, Uganda, and Togo. Given that poor leadership is clearly a significant contributing factor to many of Africa's problems, the ability of regimes to cling to power while being able to present themselves as having gone through the electoral process is deeply problematic. This is habitually compounded by the behaviour of the international community, which is often satisfied by the appearance of elections, particularly when political or economic interests outweigh any real commitment to democracy in Africa. Vote-rigging, manipulation of the press, outright fraud, and the boycotting of the elections by opposition parties have all helped serve the interest of those involved.

In fact, there are four broad models by which elites bent on maintaining their leadership prerogatives may cling onto power, even if and when elections are held. First, by discrediting the opposition as being tribalists or stooges of foreign interests (Zimbabwe being a prime example). Second, by making concessions that legitimate the process just enough to secure approval but which uphold the old order (Cameroon and Togo). Third, by allowing elections, but with the intention to keep opposition forces distracted while those in power seek the backing of the people (Benin, DRC). Finally, by going on the offensive during the run up to the elections by accusing opposition figures of corruption or treason (Malawi and Zambia). All of these processes contaminate the development of a viable electoral system, disarm the opposition, and demonstrate that those leaders who reject the idea that their power is finite will find a variety of ways to circumscribe democracy to suit their requirements.

Corruption has of course given rise to incumbents utilizing state funds to underwrite their re-election. Elections are expensive and running a campaign requires a candidate to have access to funds. This is not particular to Africa, but the context means that various malpractices appear common in elections across the continent. Exploiting state resources to further activities during the election campaign, such as using government vehicles to convey candidates and party activists, misappropriating office equipment belonging to the state, and effectively monopolizing the publicly owned media are all familiar practices. Other ways money plays a role in elections is through straight out bribery of electors; in some countries, it is quite typical that funds are utilized to buy votes. This may be through the direct distribution of hard cash or other types of compensation. The dissemination of T-shirts, small amounts of livestock, and other favours helps secure votes, particularly in the rural areas.

Alternative techniques incumbent elites may utilize to engender funds to support their election campaign consist of tapping businesspersons or other prominent citizens for 'loans', with the expectation that if elected, favours will have to be returned. In Ghana's 1992, Cameroon's 1997, and Benin's 2011 presidential elections, it was reported that candidates were backed by clusters of businessmen who delivered substantial contributions to fund electoral campaigns. After the election, these self-same donors coincidentally benefited from government policies. Elsewhere, donors may propose individuals to oversee certain governmental offices through which benefits are expected to accrue. The ministries of trade, agriculture, and health, as well as customs and excise, are particularly vulnerable to this sort of dynamic, but given that all state ministries tend to involve substantial public procurements, a proliferation of 'tendertrepreneurs' may occur. Setting aside the obvious corruption that will then take place, the whole process can be deeply problematic for governance given that the appointment of individuals to managerial positions in the state apparatus may then be based on willingness to play the game and not on competence.

The overall effect of the aforementioned practices results in an unfair political arena when it comes to elections. If successful, the actors involved in such chicanery do not need to resort to violence or open electoral fraud to stay in power. Instead, the uneven playing field makes it deeply problematic for the other political parties to compete on an equal footing. Here, incumbent abuse of the state produces such inequalities with regard to access to resources, media, and state institutions that the opposition's capacity to organize and contest for public office is gravely compromised. Access to state institutions is considered significant as a skewed playing field is created when incumbents control the judiciary, electoral authorities, electoral systems, and other independent arbiters through deployment, bribery, and intimidation, or a refusal to consider necessary reforms. These are the institutions that should ensure accountability and should act as impartial umpires in the game of politics.

It is no surprise then that incumbent dominant parties win on a recurring basis as their advantages blatantly skew the electoral playing field in their favour. These disparities are actively instigated and fostered by the ruling party as a means of securing power within a constitutional setting that requires multiparty politics as an organizing principle. The effects of these practices on the growth and strengthening of democracy may be profound. Candidates may not be voted into office on the basis of their skills or developmental vision for the country, but rather on how much money is expended, particularly if this is then linked to identity politics. In such cases, it is the government bodies and other institutions whose inability to safeguard a clean election undermines the governance structures overall. This further contributes to malgovernance and underperformance by the state.

It is obvious that the behaviour of political actors in some parts of Africa nullifies the potential of a movement towards transformed governance that might benefit the masses. Through preserving corrupted electoral processes, they weaken the possibility for change by ensuring that their individual rule and the patron–client networks which underpin their positions continue. A further way this may contribute to undermining democracy is that the elites' political chicanery may stimulate societal tensions (often expressed through identity) which are then thrown back in the faces of the opposition as 'proof' that multiparty politics is not suited to the African condition and only engenders tribalism, inter-religious conflicts, and exacerbates regional tensions. All of these pathologies have been used by various African leaders at one time or another to argue that liberal democracy cannot work in Africa. Uganda's Yoweri Museveni is perhaps the most famous contemporary exponent of this thesis, which of course then conveniently legitimizes the fact that he has been in power since 1986. In countries where societal tensions are high and political violence never far away, an Africanized version of *après nous, le deluge* can (perhaps understandably) appear convincing.

Evidence of progress

Although multiple challenges to multiparty democracy exist in Africa, it is however clear that over time it has been possible to hold authority to account and that, in general, African polities have experienced a relative improvement since the onset of democratization. Not least is the fact that multiparty elections have established a norm of peacefully replacing political leaders. This has been significant, as, although there are exceptions, the sort of long-lasting regimes that stayed in power interminably have declined in number. Previously, a coup was perhaps the only way to unseat an incumbent. However, now political space has opened up that allows the alternation of power without violence. The fact that state leadership may end through democratic means and because of the exercise of the public's voice, rather than through the actions of the military, is a substantial advance on previous patterns.

Certainly, while the results of the plethora of elections are not uniform across the continent, the consequences of multiparty elections have nonetheless borne fruit in confronting and, in various cases, ending the sort of openly authoritarian regimes that existed previously. In addition to the immediate outcomes of multiparty elections, perhaps the most important outcome can be found in the progressive changes that have occurred in the political culture of various countries that have experienced the holding of elections over a period of time. Certainly the practice of democracy in Africa is not perfect (and where is it perfect?) but most African states today operate much more openly than those before the 1990s.

The institutionalization of electoral systems has been accompanied by growing liberalization of the media, a growth in civic organizations, and the development of competitive politics. Citizens within countries who have experienced such changes are less likely to tolerate autocracy and more prone to hold officials to account. In this respect, it is important to note that the adoption of these ethics cannot be easily rolled back and, in the long-run, the pressure for these principles to be realized may be the stimulus for deeper reform. In other words, elections do not have to be perfectly free and fair to have democratizing properties; the mere holding of elections can encourage democratic awareness and a gradual emboldening of thinking and discourse with the control of political elites. Repeated democratic encounters through elections enhance the democratic learning process. Of course, in some countries, this is fragile, and destructive patron–client practices have not been eradicated. However, the relatively open political arena that encourages elections, opposition, and public debates also generates the prospects for democratic values to develop.

Final comments

Where governments have been elected, they have faced the same problems of unequal terms of trade, foreign debts, run-down agricultural systems, dependence on a limited range of export crops or minerals, poverty for the majority, inefficient bureaucratic systems, corruption, and political systems based on patronage politics. African democracies are thus distinct in the sense that, despite all the many hurdles, many have managed to make important progress towards instituting relatively stable and accountable multiparty structures. Although Freedom House's figures may appear discouraging, it should be remembered that around a quarter of African states are now 'free'. That is, a substantial fraction of the continent *is* democratizing, albeit unevenly. Despite all the myriad problems, parts of the continent demonstrate that even the most underdeveloped and fragile countries do not necessarily have to endure autocratic rule without end.

Moving forward, it is most likely that African politics is going to continue to be a mixed bag in terms of the quality of governance and the levels of democracy. Given the size of the continent, this is to be expected and there is not just one Africa. Nevertheless, even here, upsets can and do happen. Although the Arab Spring has not materialized in Africa, complacent despots such as Blaise Compaoré in Burkina Faso and Yahya Jammeh in The Gambia have both in recent times been replaced (after twenty-seven and twenty-three years of personal dictatorships, respectively). Elsewhere, there have been cases of widespread public reaction against leaders who have sought to stay in power, such as Zambia's Frederick Chiluba and Malawi's Bakili Muluzi. Both tried to change the constitution to allow themselves to stay in office; both failed in their efforts when the citizens rose up and objected. The ongoing upheaval in Burundi was sparked by Pierre Nkurunziza's successful bid to extend his term. Finally, as this book was being written, for the first time in African history, an opposition court challenge against a presidential election succeeded, when the Supreme Court announced as null and void the 2017 presidential elections in Kenya. In all cases, the reaction of the public has not been cowed by the authorities, which would have mostly been the case prior to the 1990s. Clearly, something has changed. In an era of improved communications and greater access to information, democratic impulses and the demand for accountability are likely to develop further. The youth (Africa has the youngest population in the world, with 200 million people aged between 15 and 24) are increasingly connected. The days of the Idi Amins, Mobutu Sese Sekos, and Charles Taylors are largely over.

Chapter 9
Africa's international relations

Despite the myth of marginality and irrelevance, Africa has always played an important—often vital—role in international politics. The slave trade, the 'Scramble for Africa' and subsequent colonial period, the proxy wars of the Cold War, and the increasing importance of the continent's natural resources all demonstrate how significant Africa has been to the wider global political economy. There has been a constant flow of ideas, material goods, and political contacts between Africa, Europe, and Asia since ancient times. Indeed, the continent's extra-African political and economic ties were mature long before European people began 'discovering' Africa. The continent has never been a passive bystander, devoid of agency and acted upon. Rather, an intriguing aspect of the continent's engagement with global processes is the way in which individuals or groups have profited from the situation of dependence on external resources, tactically using these relations for their own interests, primarily through appropriating resources and authority.

Prior to colonialism, this role of extraversion was performed by those Africans who profited from the slave trade and who engaged in other forms of commerce with the Europeans and Arabs. During colonialism, intermediaries operated within African societies to facilitate the exploitation of the continent for the benefit of the colonial powers. Whether these were local chiefs, compradors acting as a link between African trade and foreign firms, or colonial civil servants, they all acted to facilitate their country's own subjugation. At independence, new roles were developed which were in effect the continuation of these trends. Amilcar Cabral, the great Guinea-Bissauian intellectual and freedom fighter, noted this trend:

> To retain the power which national liberation puts in its hands, the petty bourgeoisie has only one path: to give free rein to its natural tendencies to become more bourgeois, to permit the development of a bureaucratic and intermediary bourgeoisie in the commercial cycle, in order to transform itself into a national pseudo-bourgeoisie.

Cabral argued that only if this new elite possessed sufficient ideological consciousness to commit suicide as a class and identify with the broad population would neo-colonialism be avoided. However, as is evident, ruling elites across the continent have taken advantage of their dependence, turning it into a resource for themselves and their cliques. Classic examples would be through rent-seeking, appropriating development assistance, exploiting the support for democratization by the West for their own gains, and, most recently, positioning themselves as allies in the global counter-terrorism effort. In all such examples, African leaders have proven to be remarkably skilful in exploiting external factors and the continent's relationship to the world system.

Certainly, the political and economic structures introduced by European colonialism positioned Africa in a certain way, restructuring domestic systems and putting the continent in a structurally dependent situation globally. At independence, this was inherited by the newly independent states and continued by the political elites who governed the new countries. Very few made any serious efforts to address the structures of dependency. African states' dependent position in the global system is both objective and subjective. It is objective in the sense that historical processes have established the continent in the global division of labour as an exporter of primary commodities and an importer of finished goods, and this has had a disastrous impact upon the continent's progress. It is subjective in the sense that overall, African leaders have not sought true independence. The way in which their countries are dependent, even though this damages their citizens and reproduces dependency, benefits the political and economic elites. The in-built incentive is thus to maintain the position of dependence that upholds the inflow of resources and power granted to incumbents, but with very little progress in terms of development or political maturity.

Many of these tendencies stem from the nature of the patron–client system that typifies much of political practice in Africa. The type of governance in large parts of the continent and how it combines with external processes is essential to understand if we wish to comprehend the diplomatic practices, global interactions, and broad international relations of Africa. Many African states only possess quasi-statehood—while they enjoy recognition and support from the international system of states, many are unable to sustain themselves internally and practise neo-patrimonial forms of governance antithetical to broad-based development. In short, African independence saw an international regime of juridical sovereignty incorporating (and then maintaining) weak states that lacked empirical sovereignty and that would almost certainly not have survived in previous historical periods. The effects of the Cold War in stimulating this milieu cannot be underestimated. The response from African elites presiding over such entities was to pursue a policy of extraversion—the utilization of external resources and political support to maintain power and sustain their patronage networks.

Acknowledgement of the sovereign status of many African state formations, however dysfunctional and fictitious, has allowed and even encouraged the current situation whereby many African citizens are materially worse off than they were under colonialism. Gaining control of an African state immediately supplies recognition and prestige from the outside world and provides external diplomatic backing and access to aid. This then further lubricates the patronage networks on which the state is predicated. In addition, assuming office automatically leads to membership in an elite club of African rulers who, as has been repeatedly demonstrated, band together for mutual support and protection against both external threats and, regrettably, domestic opposition to their rule. Such recognition, be it external or intra-African, is based on a concept of sovereignty that grants opportunities to rulers of even the most dysfunctional and weakest states. The use and abuse of the notion of sovereignty also allows an assortment of non-African actors to successfully construct commercial and military alliances with state leaders and their courtiers as well as with private corporations.

Many state elites in Africa have used the mantle of sovereignty not to promote the collective good but to bolster their own patronage networks and to weaken those of potential challengers. The international system is complicit in this charade. Malgovernance is aided—even perpetuated—on the continent by the doctrines of sovereignty and non-interference, and it is no coincidence that Africa's elites are among the most enthusiastic defenders of these principles. This remains the case, despite the AU's ostensible claim to provide an increased scope for intervention.

Even allegedly omnipotent international agencies such as the IMF and the World Bank have failed in achieving meaningful results in most African countries vis-à-vis their reform projects, as African governments have fought tooth and nail to protect their positions. Subversion has led to partial reform where there are considerable gaps between stated and actual commitments to reform. This is because donor-supported reforms have within them measures that would cut considerably the opportunities for informal manipulation over economic resources, rent-seeking, and the ability to show favour to clients by state actors.

Thus what occurs is the partial reform syndrome where aid-recipient administrations manipulate the reform process in order to protect their patron–client bases. Partial reform allows African elites to cast themselves as 'responsible partners' and in doing so has stimulated increased flows of aid. However, donor funding may improve access to education and health. Moral hazard emerges whereby undesirable behaviour by state elites is in danger of being stimulated—however unintentionally—because elites know that their mistakes or inappropriate behaviour such as corruption, excessive military spending, and so on will be covered by the ambiguous efforts of international organizations and non-governmental organization. Equally so, the project to transform Africa's authoritarian politics into workable democracies has largely stalled—and in many cases the donors do not seem to mind too much.

Implications for Africa's international relations

As the processes outlined previously have unfolded since independence, many African states have increasingly succumbed to modes of governance where the elites (invariably in alliance with non-African partners) have effectively undermined the formal and institutionalized structures of their own states. This process involved both internal and international elements. The informalization of politics and institutional processes has resulted in the multiplying of informal markets, popular survival strategies (increasingly operationalized through emigration), forms of privatization that depend on the patronage and largesse of diverse global actors, and, in some extreme cases, the criminalization of the very state itself. Often, such a 'rolling back of the state' has gone hand in hand with the privatization strictures of the international financial institutions, though such outcomes are no doubt quite different from what the donor community had envisioned when it promoted liberalization as the way to 'set the market free'.

An international relations of questionable statehoods across Africa is of profound importance for any discussion of the continent's interactions with the world. In fact, while the Western-derived (and approved) state model has increasingly foundered, Africans, through a dialectic of structural pressures and their own political agency, have continually interacted with the world in ways that accommodate ideas of personal and communal progress and order. Although these concepts are defined in ways that do not necessarily resonate with dominant liberal approaches, they nonetheless represent African agency: they are rational and careful responses to the irresponsibility of the continent's elites and the stress placed on Africa by global pressures. Private (and occasionally public) corporations, diasporic communities, sportsmen and -women, musical collaboration, and criminal networks all flourish next to, together with, and 'beneath' the more readily observable state-to-state interactions that make up Africa's international relations.

Interests, old and new

Currently, Africa is increasingly important in international relations and is attracting more and more interest from a huge array of actors at a scale perhaps not witnessed since the original Scramble for Africa. The rise of China in Africa has particularly caught the attention of many, but other emerging powers such as India, Brazil, Russia, Turkey, and so on have all gone into Africa in the last two decades in a major way; China is now Africa's largest trading partner. A generalized critique of this development is that these countries do not particularly exert themselves in promoting democracy and human rights. While this may be so, it would be erroneous to cast the West as virtuous in this regard. Western policy towards the continent has been and remains incredibly cynical and appeals to democracy are usually directed at those leaders who don't toe the line or who start to become a liability for Western interests.

Surprisingly, the United States does not have a particularly strong presence in Africa. For many years, the United States perceived few if any direct strategic or economic interests in Africa, and engagement with the region was largely defined by the logic of the Cold War.

After 9/11, American policy has been increasingly securitized and much of Washington's involvement in Africa is to do with counter-terrorism. The formation in 2007 under the George W. Bush administration of the United States Africa Command (AFRICOM) exemplified this focus. Although mainly a bureaucratic move aimed at better coordinating American military activities in Africa, it has generated huge suspicions. The election of Barack Obama did not change matters substantially. Obama's engagement with Africa was dominated by a perceived increase in terrorist activities in Africa, dealing with the dramatic engagement of China (and others) with the continent, and African oil. The latter however rapidly became less important as developments in shale gas production and other sources of energy acted as a supply shock that transformed the energy market and led to a collapse in American imports of African oil. This is a remarkable turnaround and is bound to have profound implications for American interests in Africa. The continent in any case was not a priority for Obama. It took nine months for an American ambassador to the AU to be in post, and a strategy towards Africa was not released until June 2012 (Obama assumed power in January 2009). Obama only visited Africa rarely, with brief visits to Egypt and Ghana during his first year in office (the latter visit lasted less than twenty-four hours). Obama in fact only visited his father's homeland of Kenya in mid-2015, six years after he became president (Figure 8). In contrast, in May 2011 he visited Moneygall in Ireland, the birthplace of his great-great-great-grandfather on his mother's side. As for Donald Trump, interest in Africa is minimal and his tweets about the continent have typically dismissed it as a corruption-ridden, crime-infested basket case—or worse.

8. **Obama visiting Africa.**

Turning to a rather more proactive set of relations, of all the former colonial powers, France alone has actively retained strong direct interests in Africa. At the same time, however, Paris has tolerated very high levels of corruption and mismanagement among its allies in Africa. Uniquely, there is an actual neologism for France's role in Africa: *Françafrique*. This term was originally a positive expression, crafted by President Houphouët-Boigny of Côte d'Ivoire denoting France's historically close ties with Africa. However, the term in contemporary usage has very negative and neo-colonial connotations and captures a very murky world that links African 'big men' to the French political and business elites, with direct personal links lubricating various transactions. France maintains military bases in Africa, and has repeatedly interfered militarily in African politics, usually to shore up a pro-French incumbent or to facilitate the removal of a president who has not paid sufficient attention to French requirements. In turn, French political parties have received donations from corrupt African leaders, and French companies (especially in the oil industry) are given extraordinary privileges. For France, Africa is a ticket to world-power status and an ally to block the global expansionism of English and *les Anglo-Saxons*. This led to the debacle in Rwanda where France ended up supporting those who had committed the genocide. Africa is an ally to secure votes at the UN for French positions; France's involvement in Africa and its role there bolster its claims that it is a peer of other major European and global powers. In short, France has been able to hold onto some shreds of its former empire, particularly in Africa, mainly by playing a re-fashioned form of indirect rule, only mindful of some of the sensitivities of African independence.

For the United Kingdom's part, although it has a substantial colonial history, Britain's policies towards Africa have not been a priority. The real focus of British foreign policy has always been on UK–US relations (and perhaps the EU). Since independence was granted to its African colonies, every British government has generally seen Africa as a source of trouble or a problem to be solved, with Africa only temporarily featuring in diplomatic priorities. These would include, *inter alia*, Rhodesia (1965–80) and the 'kith and kin' problem; Biafra (1967–70) and keeping Nigeria together; South Africa in 1980s and defending the apartheid state; Zimbabwe in the 2000s and responding to Robert Mugabe's 'land reforms'; and, in 2005, Britain's chairmanship of the G-8 and the European Union and the whole 'Make Poverty History' moment. These have all proven ultimately rather transitory. Furthermore, under Labour, the Department for International Development (DfID) was established, which quickly became central in the British relationship with Africa. The target of spending of 0.7 per cent of GDP has been adopted and is now central to Anglo-African relations. Consequently, Africa has been virtually handed over to the DfID in terms of policy. The DfID has huge resources and a guaranteed yearly increase in budget, while the Foreign Office faces continuous cuts. In general, people whose prime job is to watch and analyse for British national interests do not lead British diplomatic missions in Africa. Rather, the United Kingdom is largely represented by officials primarily concerned with pushing aid onto Africa. While, obviously, various African elites are appreciative of such largesse, the signal sent by London currently is that Africa is regarded in London as a place dependent on aid, rather than something approaching equality.

This last trend leads us to the question of aid in the continent's international relations. By the late 1970s, many African economies were in crisis. The world had seen a big increase in oil prices, an increase in global interest rates, a worldwide recession, and decreasing prices for other commodities. These factors, coupled with waste, corruption, mismanagement, and huge loans accrued when the commodity prices were high meant that while in 1970 sub-Saharan Africa's debt was $9 billion, by 1978 it has reached $60 billion. In response, the World Bank identified the key problem as the post-colonial state, and the solution was less state and more market. The global context of Thatcherism and Reaganomics was critical in influencing the international financial institutions introducing 'structural adjustment programmes' (SAPs), a generic term used to describe a package of measures which the IMF, World Bank, and individual Western aid donors imposed on developing countries. Simply put, recipient countries had to agree to various policies before being granted loans to finance deficit on their balance of payments and/or finance new projects for further economic or social development. These were known as 'conditionalities' and were essentially made up of five ingredients: the promotion of outward-oriented growth; the expansion of the private sector as the growth process's driving force; the removal of barriers to international capital flows; diminishing the role of the state; and de-regulation and re-structuring of the domestic labour market.

This imposition of export-led growth strategies for resolving the debt crisis turned out to be problematic due to commodity price issues, notably that many African producers hugely increased their production, only to see foreign-exchange earnings fall as the terms of trade declined and an over-production of commodities flooded the market. The social effects of SAPs were disastrous:

average incomes fell by 20 per cent during the 1980s, open unemployment quadrupled to a hundred million, investment into Africa fell to levels which were lower than in 1970, and Africa's share of world markets fell by half. A study by the World Bank itself in 2000 concluded that 'growth of per-capita income for a typical developing country during the 1980s and 1990s was zero'; and, in 2000, the Joint Economic Committee of the US Congress found a failure rate of 73 per cent for all World Bank sponsored projects in Africa.

SAPs were strongly criticized, and subsequently developing countries from 1999 onwards have been encouraged by the World Bank to draw up Poverty Reduction Strategy Papers (PRSPs) instead. The IMF in turn replaced its Enhanced Structural Adjustment Facility (ESAF) with the Poverty Reduction and Growth Facility (PRGF), essentially PRSP-compliant. PRSPs are intended to be the basis for all foreign aid to poor countries and all countries are required to produce a PRSP as a basis for concessional lending from the IMF or Bank. While promoted as qualitatively different from SAPs, little has changed in terms of the Fund's and the Bank's negotiating style: loan negotiations are conducted behind closed doors, lacking disclosure, public involvement, and oversight. While the IMF has engaged in the process of streamlining conditionality (and the World Bank claims to be doing this too, unofficially) there is little evidence to date that freedom of choice for borrowing countries has increased. Furthermore, the macro-economic framework is still essentially neo-liberal and the same economists (from the same school of Economics) dominate. Of course, whether African countries should be required to pay off debt contracted by non-democratic regimes and when the lenders knew the nature of the governments they were lending to is a moot point.

This latter issue brings us to a rather remarkable state of affairs. Far from the popular image of the continent as supplicatory to the benevolent West, Africa in fact is a net global creditor by around $41 billion per year. A report in 2017 by *Global Justice Now* estimated that the total amount going into sub-Saharan Africa was $161.6 billion, while the total amount going out was $202.9 billion. These drainages included debt repayments by governments and the private sector ($18 billion per year, while aid coming in was $19.7 billion), multinational corporation profits ($32.4 billion), the 'brain drain' effect, illegal logging, fishing and poaching, and sundry costs associated with climate change. Illicit financial outflows such as companies misreporting the value of imports and exports totalled around $67.6 billion. While the methodology of colonial plunder may have changed, its essential character remains the same.

African unity

The aspiration to African unity has long been held and is captured in the concept of Pan-Africanism. This is a political, cultural, and intellectual tradition that regards Africa, Africans, and African descendants as a unit. The aim has always been the regeneration and unification of Africa and is based on the idea that Africa can only be free and a political power in the world if it is united. Pan-Africanism was conceived by people of African descent in the Caribbean and in the United States, and can be traced back to the 18th century, developed in response to their alienation and loss of identity through slavery and their everyday experiences of racism in the New World.

As Africa was about to embark on its independence path, the figure of Kwame Nkrumah emerged to become the voice and organizing force of Pan-Africanism. In the late 1940s and 1950s, Nkrumah promoted the idea of an independent West African Federation as the first step towards a United States of Africa. Crucially, in March 1957, he became leader of the newly independent state of Ghana (Figure 9), and one of his first thoughts was to use his new position to work towards uniting the continent. The key question at this time was whether African

9. Kwame Nkrumah at Ghana independence celebrations.

colonial territories should continentally pursue unity or, rather, discrete national independence. In general, the former French colonies and conservative leaders elsewhere were much less keen on the idea of unity, preferring to retain their ties with the colonial powers. After much debate and intrigue, instead of the United States of Africa dreamed of by Nkrumah, the Organization of African Unity (OAU) came into being on 25 May 1963, with a headquarters in Addis Ababa. The OAU charter was essentially functional, and reflected a compromise between the concept of a loose association of states and the federal idea of a united Africa. Subsequently, the OAU was an ineffective collection of nation-states, primarily focused on defending Africa's newly gained sovereignty. It swiftly degenerated into a club for African presidents to band together, losing much of its credibility. Although the OAU retained in its constitution the ideal of Pan-Africanism, in practice this remained a moribund, forgotten project.

The African Union (AU) was established in 2002 as the successor to the OAU (Figure 10). The aim of the AU is to promote continental integration and development, as well as peace and security and stability. Unlike the OAU, the AU has been quite proactive in seeking to resolve conflicts and has moved away from the stance of non-interference to one of non-indifference to the violation of human rights. Although sovereignty remains highly respected, the AU is arguably less of an old boys' club, and has at times taken a robust position against military coups (now forbidden under the AU charter) and some contraventions of rights. However, it is axiomatic that organizations are only as strong as their members, and despite the AU's good intentions it remains hidebound by the behaviour and attitude of its constituent members. Perhaps most cynically, the AU's members do not believe in their own organization, refusing to pay their membership fees, and thus

10. African Union headquarters, Addis Ababa.

crippling the AU's effectiveness, leaving the AU dependent on donors. Emblematically, when the Chinese built the $200-million AU headquarters in Addis Ababa in 2012, this was celebrated as a new era for Africa, rather than a source of shame that the fifty-plus members of the organization could not (or would not) pay for their own headquarters. Subsequent revelations in 2018 regarding Chinese spying activities within the new building merely added to the embarrassment.

Taking a step down from the continental level, as is well-known, the map of Africa is full of straight-line boundaries and rather nonsensical borders, the result mainly of the Berlin Conference in 1885. Consequently, since the 1960s, regionalization has been conceived as a way in which more rational economic units, with larger markets and economies of scale for investment and production, might be constructed. Regional integration then has been seen moving towards more effective economic frameworks within which to correct some of negatives associated with the colonial carving up of the continent. Regionalism in Africa then has been pursued for two key reasons: to enhance political unity (i.e. the Pan-African agenda) and economic rationality to foster growth and development. The goal has been to maximize the internal and external economic, political, social, and cultural benefits of interaction.

A remarkable feature of the continent is that African countries do not trade much among themselves. Crossing borders in Africa is the most expensive in the world and the cost of transporting goods in Africa is the highest. Many African transport networks are notorious for being severely under-maintained and thus massively slowing down the transportation of produce. Note here that during the 1970s and 1980s, the value of Africa's road stock deteriorated by an estimated $45 billion while an investment of $12 billion in maintenance would have avoided this. Equally, Africa's transport networks exhibit classical colonial geographies; the vast majority of the continent's railways, for instance, even to this day, go from the hinterland to the coast. Extraction remains the prime purpose of such routes and internal trade is a secondary consideration.

Earlier attempts at implementing regional market integration were inward looking and generally relied on import substitution industrialization policies whereby domestic production was highly protected from imported competition. Though there were some gains in the manufacturing sector, the ultimate result was that many African countries by the 1980s were producing high-priced but inefficient products, which proved to be no substitute for cheaper more efficient imports. The 1980s witnessed a change in strategy, with the SAPs and forced liberalization. However, SAPs *discouraged* regional market integration and instead encouraged African countries to unilaterally open their markets in the name of efficiency and competition. Apart from the doubtful wisdom of reproducing Africa's external dependency, internal logics intervened as regimes that were already losing revenue from liberalization policies were in no mood to implement free trade, even at the regional level.

This resistance has continued today and serves to undermine deeper integration. Simply put, regionalization does not make sense in a neo-patrimonial context. Borders represent opportunities, and customs regulations, import/export licences, visas, etc. are the devices of governmental control and sources of resource extraction. A set of informal rules as to how one crosses the border exists in most African settings and a part of the game is that these rules can be manipulated by officials to sustain their control and maintain rent-seeking abilities for personal profit and regime survival through the issuing of import licences, permits, and so on. Obtaining jobs at the border in government employment is a resource and part of the patronage system. Equally, discrepancies in market value make smuggling across borders extremely profitable. For instance, in Togo oil smuggled in from Nigeria costs much less than legitimate oil bought from

Togo's licensed filling stations. Free trade as proposed by the dominant regionalization model would mean that smugglers and officials with a willingness to take the risk would no longer be rewarded, while prices on the street might go up, affecting the population. Thus, existing networks share a strong interest in the preservation of good relations between neighbouring states but also in the maintenance of customs and tariff barriers. The way in which politics is characterized by patronage politics and informalization thus again emerges and shapes how continental integration is affected. Overcoming this conundrum is extremely difficult and will certainly be a major challenge for the ambitious African Continental Free Trade Agreement (AfCFTA), which was announced with much fanfare in 2018.

References

Chapter 1: Introduction to Africa and its politics

Tim Kelsall, 'Shop Windows and Smoke-Filled Rooms: Governance and the Re-Politicisation of Tanzania', *Journal of Modern African Studies*, vol. 40, no. 4, 2002, pp. 597–619.

Angus Maddison, *The World Economy: A Millennial Perspective*. Paris: OECD Publishing, 2006, p. 126.

Will Reno, *Corruption and State Politics in Sierra Leone*. Cambridge: Cambridge University Press, 1995.

Walter Rodney, *How Europe Underdeveloped Africa*. London: Bogle-L'Ouverture Publications, 1972.

Ricardo Soares de Oliveira, *Oil and Politics in the Gulf of Guinea*. London: Hurst, 2008.

Emmanuel Terray, 'Le climatiseur et la veranda', *Afrique plurielle, Afrique actuelle. Hommage à Georges Balandier*. Paris: Karthala, 1986.

Chapter 2: Pre-colonial political systems and colonialism

Kenneth Good, 'Settler Colonialism: Economic Development and Class Formation', *Journal of Modern African Studies*, vol. 14, no. 4, 1976, pp. 597–620.

Adam Hochschild, *King Leopold's Ghost: A Story of Greed, Terror and Heroism in Colonial Africa*. Boston, MA: Mariner Books, 1998.

I.B. Kake, 'The Slave Trade and the Population Drain from Black Africa to North Africa and the Middle East', *The African Slave Trade from the Fifteenth to the Nineteenth Century*. Paris: UNESCO, 1979, pp. 164–74.

Frederick Lugard, *The Dual Mandate in British Tropical Africa*. London: Frank Cass, 1965, p. 94.

Nathan Nunn, 'The Long-Term Effects of Africa's Slave Trades', *Quarterly Journal of Economics*, vol. 123, no. 1, 2008, pp. 139–76.

Isaac Schapera, *A Handbook of Tswana Law and Custom*. Oxford: Boydell and Brewer, 1994.

Ronald Segal, *Islam's Black Slaves: A History of Africa's Other Black Diaspora*. London: Atlantic Books, 2003.

Trans-Atlantic Slave Trade Database, www.slavevoyages.org.

Dorothy White, *Black Africa and De Gaulle: From the French Empire to Independence*. University Park, PA: Pennsylvania State Press, 1997, p. 36.

Eric Williams, *Capitalism and Slavery*. London: André Deutsch, 1964.

Chapter 3: The transfer of power and the colonial legacy

African Statistical Yearbook, Economic Commission for Africa, African Development Bank and the African Union Commission, published annually.

Kwame Nkrumah, *I Speak of Freedom: A Statement of African Ideology*. New York, NY: Praeger, 1961, p. 117.

Kwame Nkrumah, 'Neocolonialism in Africa', *The Africa Reader: Independent Africa* New York, NY: Vintage Books, 1970, pp. 217–18.

John Saul and Colin Leys, 'Sub-Saharan Africa in Global Capitalism', *Monthly Review*, vol. 51, no. 3, 1999.

Issa Shivji, *Accumulation in an African Periphery: A Theoretical Framework*. Dar es Salaam: Mkuki na Nyota Publishers, 2009, p. 59.

Crawford Young, *Ideology and Development in Africa*. New Haven, CT: Yale University Press, 1982.

Chapter 4: The primacy of patronage politics

Wale Adebanwi and Ebenezer Obadare (eds), *Democracy and Prebendal Politics in Nigeria: Critical Interpretations*. Basingstoke: Palgrave, 2013.

Bertrand Badie, *The Imported State: The Westernization of the Political Order*. Stanford, CA: Stanford University Press, 2000, p. 19.

Peter Ekeh, 'Colonialism and the Two Publics in Africa: A Theoretical Statement', *Comparative Studies in Society and History*, vol. 17, no. 1, 1975, pp. 91–112.

Richard Joseph, *Democracy and Prebendal Politics in Nigeria: The Rise and Fall of the Second Republic*. Cambridge: Cambridge University Press, 1987.

Ahmadou Kourouma, *Waiting for the Wild Beasts to Vote*. London: William Heinemann, 2003, p. 221.

Jean François Médard, 'The Underdeveloped State in Africa: Political Clientelism or Neo-patrimonialism?', in Christopher Clapham (ed.), *Private Patronage and Public Power: Political Clientelism and the Modern State*. London: Frances Pinter, 1982, pp. 162–89.

Max Weber, *Economy and Society: An Outline of Interpretive Sociology*. Berkeley: University of California Press, 1978.

Chapter 5: Women in African politics

Africa Human Development Report 2016: Accelerating Gender Equality and Women's Empowerment in Africa. New York: UNDP, 2016.

Colleen Kriger, 'Textile Production and Gender in the Sokoto Caliphate', *Journal of African History*, vol. 34, no. 3, 1993, pp. 361–401.

Aili Mari Tripp, *Women and Power in Postconflict Africa*. New York: Cambridge University Press, 2015.

Chapter 6: The role of identity in African politics

Chinua Achebe, *There Was a Country: A Personal History of Biafra*. London: Allen Lane, 2012.

Patricia Bamurangirwa, *Rwanda Yesterday*. Kibworth Beauchamp: Matador, 2013.

K.W.J. Post and Michael Vickers, *Structure and Conflict in Nigeria, 1960–65*. London: Heinemann, 1973.

Charles Seligman, *Races* of *Africa*. London: Thornton Butterworth, 1930.

Alexis de Tocqueville, *Democracy in America*. London: HarperCollins, 2007, p. 268.

Chapter 7: The military in African politics

M. Chris Alli, *The Federal Republic of Nigerian Army: The Siege of a Nation*. Lagos: Malthouse Press, 2001.

A.H.M. Kirk-Greene, *'Stay by Your Radios': Documentation for a Study of Military Government in Tropical Africa.* Leiden: Afrika-Studiecentrum, 1980.

Jonathan Powell and Clayton Thyne, 'Global Instances of Coups from 1950–Present', *Journal of Peace Research*, vol. 48, no. 2, 2011, pp. 249–59.

Chapter 8: Democracy in Africa

Thomas Callaghy, 'Politics and Vision in Africa: The Interplay of Domination, Equality and Liberty', in Patrick Chabal (ed.), *Political Domination in Africa: Reflections on the Limits of Power.* Cambridge: Cambridge University Press, 1986, p. 45.

André-Michel Essoungou, 'African Elections: Works in Progress', *Africa Renewal*, August 2011, p. 15. http://www.un.org/en/africarenewal/vol25no2-3/african-elections.html.

Freedom House, www.freedomhouse.org.

Jonathan Moyo, 'The African Renaissance: A Critical Assessment', *Southern African Political and Economic Monthly*, vol. 11, no. 7, 1998, p. 11.

Chapter 9: Africa's international relations

Jean-François Bayart, 'Africa in the World: A History of Extraversion', *African Affairs*, vol. 99, no. 395, 2000, pp. 217–67.

Amilcar Cabral, *Revolution in Guinea: An African People's Struggle.* London: Stage One, 1969, p. 80.

Christopher Clapham, *Africa and the International System: The Politics of State Survival.* Cambridge: Cambridge University Press, 1996.

William Easterly, 'The Lost Decades: Developing Countries' Stagnation in Spite of Policy Reform 1980–1998', *Journal of Economic Growth*, vol. 6, no. 2, 2001, pp. 135–57.

Global Justice Now, *Honest Accounts 2017: How the World Profits from Africa's Wealth.* London: Global Justice Now, 2017.

Joint Economic Committee, *Reform of the IMF and World Bank: Hearing Before the Joint Economic Committee Congress of the United States One Hundred Sixth Congress, Second Session, April 12, 2000.* Washington, DC: US Government Printing Office, 2000.

Victor Le Vine, *Politics in Francophone Africa*. Boulder, CO: Lynne Rienner, 2004.

Karl Polanyi Levitt, 'Linkage and Vulnerability: The "Debt Crisis" in Latin America and Africa', in Bonnie Campbell (ed.), *Political Dimensions of the International Debt Crisis*. London: Palgrave Macmillan, 1989.

Kenna Owoh, 'Fragmenting Health Care: The World Bank Prescription for Africa', *Alternatives*, vol. 21, no. 2, 1996, pp. 211–37.

Nicholas van de Walle, *African Economies and the Politics of Permanent Crisis 1979–1999*. Cambridge: Cambridge University Press, 2001.

François-Xavier Verschave, *La Françafrique. Le plus long scandale de la République*. Paris: Éditions Stock, 1998.

World Bank, *Road Deterioration in Developing Countries: Causes and Remedies*. Washington, DC: World Bank, 1998.

References

Further reading

For an excellent overview of developments in Africa since the continent formally regained its independence, see Paul Nugent, *Africa Since Independence*, 2nd edition. Basingstoke: Palgrave, 2012.

Africa has a rich and growing canon of literature, most dealing with contemporary issues in some way or another. They are a good way of gaining an African insight into some of the topics discussed in this book. Some suggested novels are:

Ahmadou Kourouma, *Waiting for the Wild Beast to Vote*. London: Vintage, 2004. An outstanding satire on Africa's big men and the political systems they run.

Chinua Achebe, *Things Fall Apart*. London: Heinemann, 1958. Portrays the collision of African and European cultures in human terms and the changes introduced into Africa by colonial rule.

Ayi Kwei Armah, *The Beautyful Ones Are Not Yet Born*. Boston, MA: Houghton, Mifflin, 1968. A railway clerk tries to resist the pressures from both his family and society to indulge in corruption.

Mariama Ba, *So Long a Letter*. London: Heinemann, 2008. A poignant look at the customs and duties facing women in Senegal.

Biyi Bandele-Thomas, *The Sympathetic Undertaker and Other Dreams*. London: Heinemann, 1993. Exposes the institutionalized brutality of politics in Nigeria.

Amma Darko, *Beyond the Horizon*. London: Heinemann, 1995. Portrays the callous exploitation of African women both on the continent and in Europe.

Ngũgĩ wa Thiong'o, *Wizard of the Crow*. London: Vintage, 2006. A burlesque on the malgovernance in some African states.

Buchi Emecheta, *The Joys of Motherhood*. London: Heinemann, 2008. A thought provoking and insightful look on life for women in Nigeria.

Amu Djoleto, *Money Galore*. London: Heinemann, 1986. A satire depicting the corruption, dishonesty, and immorality in postcolonial Ghana.

Chapter 1: Introduction to Africa and its politics

Claude Ake, *A Political Economy of Africa*. Harlow: Longman, 1981.

Bill Freund, *The Making of Contemporary Africa: The Development of African Society Since 1800*. London: Macmillan, 1984.

Tatah Mentan, *The State in Africa: An Analysis of Impacts of Historical Trajectories of Global Capitalist Expansion and Domination in the Continent*. Bamenda: Langaa, 2010.

Walter Rodney, *How Europe Underdeveloped Africa*. London: Bogle-L'Ouverture Publications, 1972.

Severine Rugumanu, *Globalization Demystified: Africa's Possible Development Futures*. Dar es Salaam: University of Dar es Salaam Press, 2005.

Issa Shivji, *Accumulation in an African Periphery: A Theoretical Framework*. Dar es Salaam: Mkuki na Nyota, 2009.

Paul Tiyambe Zeleza, *Africa's Resurgence: Domestic, Global and Diasporic Transformations*. Los Angeles, CA: Tsehai Publishers, 2014.

Chapter 2: Pre-colonial political systems and colonialism

J.F. Ade Ajayi (ed.), *UNESCO General History of Africa*, vol. VI: *Africa in the Nineteenth Century Until the 1880s*. London: James Currey, 1998.

A. Adu Boahen, *African Perspectives on Colonialism*. Baltimore, MD: Johns Hopkins University Press, 1987.

A. Adu Boahen (ed.), *UNESCO General History of Africa*, vol. VII: *Africa Under Colonial Domination, 1880–1935*. London: James Currey, 1990.

Aimé Césaire, *Discourse on Colonialism*. New York: Monthly Review Press, 2001.

Frantz Fanon, *Black Skin, White Masks*. New York: Grove Press, 2008.

Ivan Hrbek (ed.), *UNESCO General History of Africa*, vol. III: *Africa From the Seventh to the Eleventh Century*. London: James Currey, 1992.

Joseph Ki-Zerbo and D. Niane (eds), *UNESCO General History of Africa*, vol. IV: *Africa From the Twelfth to the Sixteenth Century*. London: James Currey, 1997.

G. Mokhtar (ed.), *UNESCO General History of Africa*, vol. II: *Ancient Civilizations of Africa*. London: James Currey, 1990.

B.A. Ogot (ed.), *UNESCO General History of Africa*, vol. V: *Africa From the Sixteenth to the Eighteenth Century*. London: James Currey, 1999.

Hugh Thomas, *The Slave Trade: The History of the Atlantic Slave Trade, 1440–1870*. London: Picador, 1997.

Chapter 3: The transfer of power and the colonial legacy

Samir Amin, *Neo-Colonialism in West Africa*. London: Penguin, 1973.

Amilcar Cabral, *Return to the Source: Selected Speeches of Amilcar Cabral*. New York: Monthly Review Press, 1973.

Toyin Falola, *The Power of African Cultures*. Rochester, NY: University of Rochester Press, 2003.

Achille Mbembe, *On the Postcolony*. Berkeley, CA: University of California Press, 2001.

Bob Moore and L.J. Butler, *Crises of Empire: Decolonisation and Europe's Imperial States, 1918–1975*. London: Bloomsbury, 2008.

Sabelo Ndlovu-Gatsheni, *Coloniality of Power in Postcolonial Africa: Myths of Declonisation*. Dakar: CODESRIA, 2013.

Kwame Nkrumah, *Neo-Colonialism: The Last Stage of Imperialism*. London: PanAf Books, 1974.

Martin Thomas, *Fight or Flight: Britain, France and their Roads from Empire*. Oxford: Oxford University Press, 2014.

Chapter 4: The primacy of patronage politics

Daniel Bach and Mamadou Gazibo (eds), *Neopatrimonialism in Africa and Beyond*. London: Routledge, 2012.

Giorgio Blundo and Jean-Pierre Olivier de Sardan, *Everyday Corruption and the State: Citizens and Public Officials in Africa*. Cape Town: David Philip, 2006.

Robert Fatton, *Predatory Rule: State and Civil Society in Africa.*
Boulder, CO: Lynne Rienner, 1992.

Robert Jackson and Carl Rosberg, *Personal Rule in Black Africa:
Prince, Autocrat, Prophet, Tyrant.* Berkeley, CA: University of
California Press, 1982.

Lucy Koechlin, *Corruption as an Empty Signifier: Politics and
Political Order in Africa.* Leiden: Brill, 2013.

Roger Tangri, *The Politics of Patronage in Africa: Parastatals,
Privatization and Private Enterprise.* Trenton, NJ: Africa
World Press, 1999.

Chapter 5: Women in African politics

Balghis Badri and Aili Mari Tripp (eds), *Women's Activism in Africa:
Struggles for Rights and Representation.* London: Zed Books, 2017.

Sylvain Boko, Mina Baliamoune-Lutz, and Sitawa Kimuna (eds),
*Women in African Development: The Challenges of Globalization
and Liberalization in the 21st Century.* Trenton, NJ: Africa
World Press, 2005.

Catherine Cole, Takyiwaa Manuh, and Stephan Miescher (eds), *Africa
After Gender?* Bloomington, IN: Indiana University Press, 2007.

Catherine Coquery-Vidrovitch, *African Women: A Modern History.*
Boulder, CO: Westview Press, 1997.

Andrea Cornwell (ed.), *Readings in Gender in Africa.* Bloomington,
IN: Indiana University Press, 2005.

Kathleen Sheldon, *African Women: Early History to the 21st Century.*
Bloomington, IN: Indiana University Press, 2017.

Aili Tripp, Isabel Casimiro, Joy Kwesiga, and Alice Mungwa, *African
Women's Movements: Transforming Political Landscapes.*
Cambridge: Cambridge University Press, 2009.

Chapter 6: The role of identity in African politics

Ansa Asamoa, *Classes and Tribalism in Ghana.* Accra: Woeli
Publishing, 2007.

Bruce Berman, Dickson Eyoh, and Will Kymlicka (eds), *Ethnicity and
Democracy in Africa.* Oxford: James Currey, 2004.

Morten Bøås and Kevin Dunn, *Politics of Origin in Africa:
Autochthony, Citizenship and Conflict.* London: Zed Books, 2013.

Aidan Campbell, *Western Primitivism: African Ethnicity: A Study on
Cultural Relations.* London: Cassell, 1997.

Jeff Haynes, *Religion and Politics in Africa*. London: Zed Books, 1996.

Edmond Keller, *Identity, Citizenship and Political Conflict in Africa*. Bloomington, IN: Indiana University Press, 2014.

Okwudiba Nnoli, *Ethnic Conflicts in Africa*. Dakar: CODESRIA, 1998.

Chapter 7: The military in African politics

Maggie Dwyer, *Soldiers in Revolt: Army Mutinies in Africa*. London: Hurst, 2017.

Ruth First, *Power in Africa*. New York: Pantheon Books, 1970.

Mathurin Houngnikpo, *Guarding the Guardians: Civil-Military Relations and Democratic Governance in Africa*. Aldershot: Ashgate, 2010.

Herbert Howe, *Ambiguous Order: Military Forces in African States*. Boulder, CO: Lynne Rienner, 2005.

Eboe Hutchful and Abdoulaye Bathily (eds), *The Military and Militarism in Africa*. Dakar: CODESRIA, 1998.

Jimmy Kandeh, *Coups from Below: Armed Subalterns and State Power in West Africa*. London: Palgrave, 2004.

T.O. Odetola, *Military Regimes and Development: A Comparative Analysis of African States*. London: Routledge, 1982.

Chapter 8: Democracy in Africa

Claude Ake, *The Feasibility of Democracy in Africa*. Dakar: CODESRIA, 2000.

Matthias Basedau, Gero Erdmann, and Andreas Mehler (eds), *Votes, Money and Violence: Political Parties and Elections in Sub-Saharan Africa*. Uppsala: Nordic Africa Institute, 2007.

Dorina Bekoe (ed.), *Voting in Fear: Electoral Violence in Sub-Saharan Africa*. Washington, DC: United States Institute of Peace, 2012.

Nic Cheeseman, *Democracy in Africa: Successes, Failures and the Struggle for Reform*. Cambridge: Cambridge University Press, 2015.

Lindberg, Staffan (ed.), *Democratization by Elections: A New Mode of Transition*. Baltimore: Johns Hopkins University Press, 2009.

Tatah Mentan, *Held Together by Pins: Liberal Democracy Under Siege in Africa*. Trenton, NJ: Africa World Press, 2007.

John Mukum Mbaku and Julius Ihonvbere (eds), *Multiparty Democracy and Political Change: Constraints to Democratization in Africa*. Trenton, NJ: Africa World Press, 2002.

Muna Ndulo (ed.), *Democratic Reform in Africa: Its Impact on Governance and Poverty Alleviation*. Oxford: James Currey, 2006.

Issa Shivji, *Where is Uhuru? Reflections on the Struggle for Democracy in Africa*. Cape Town: Pambakuza, 2009.

Ian Taylor, *NEPAD: Towards Africa's Development or Another False Start?* Boulder, CO: Lynne Rienner, 2005.

Chapter 9: Africa's international relations

Patrick Bond, *Looting Africa: The Economics of Exploitation*. London: Zed Books, 2006.

Tom Burgis, *The Looting Machine: Warlords, Tycoons, Smugglers and the Systematic Theft of Africa's Wealth*. London: William Collins, 2015.

Frederick Cooper, *Africa in the World: Capitalism, Empire and the Nation-State*. Cambridge, MA: Harvard University Press, 2014.

Stephen Ellis, *Season of Rains: Africa in the World*. London: Hurst, 2011.

John Harbeson and Donald Rothchild (eds), *Africa in World Politics: Constructing Political and Economic Order*. Boulder, CO: Westview, 2017.

Kwame Ninsin (ed.), *Globalized Africa: Political, Social and Economic Impacts*. Legon: Freedom Publications, 2002.

Ian Taylor, *China's New Role in Africa*. Boulder, CO: Lynne Rienner, 2009.

Ian Taylor, *The International Relations of Sub-Saharan Africa*. New York: Continuum, 2010.

Ian Taylor, *Africa Rising? BRICS—Diversifying Dependency*. Oxford: James Currey, 2014.

Index

V

veranda politics 2, 45

W

Williams, Eric 16
World Bank 4, 9, 111, 117, 118

Z

AFRICAN HISTORY
A Very Short Introduction
John Parker & Richard Rathbone

Essential reading for anyone interested in the African continent and the diversity of human history, this *Very Short Introduction* looks at Africa's past and reflects on the changing ways it has been imagined and represented. Key themes in current thinking about Africa's history are illustrated with a range of fascinating historical examples, drawn from over 5 millennia across this vast continent.

> 'A very well informed and sharply stated historiography . . . should be in every historiography student's kitbag. A tour de force . . . it made me think a great deal.'
>
> Terence Ranger,
> **The Bulletin of the School of Oriental and African Studies**

INTERNATIONAL RELATIONS
A Very Short Introduction
Paul Wilkinson

Of undoubtable relevance today, in a post-9-11 world of growing political tension and unease, this *Very Short Introduction* covers the topics essential to an understanding of modern international relations. Paul Wilkinson explains the theories and the practice that underlies the subject, and investigates issues ranging from foreign policy, arms control, and terrorism, to the environment and world poverty. He examines the role of organizations such as the United Nations and the European Union, as well as the influence of ethnic and religious movements and terrorist groups which also play a role in shaping the way states and governments interact. This up-to-date book is required reading for those seeking a new perspective to help untangle and decipher international events.

www.oup.com/vsi

GEOPOLITICS
A Very Short Introduction
Klaus Dodds

In certain places such as Iraq or Lebanon, moving a few feet either side of a territorial boundary can be a matter of life or death, dramatically highlighting the connections between place and politics. For a country's location and size as well as its sovereignty and resources all affect how the people that live there understand and interact with the wider world. Using wide-ranging examples, from historical maps to James Bond films and the rhetoric of political leaders like Churchill and George W. Bush, this Very Short Introduction shows why, for a full understanding of contemporary global politics, it is not just smart - it is essential - to be geopolitical.

'Engrossing study of a complex topic.'

Mick Herron, Geographical.

ISLAMIC HISTORY
A Very Short Introduction
Adam J. Silverstein

Does history matter? This book argues not that history matters, but that Islamic history does. This *Very Short Introduction* introduces the story of Islamic history; the controversies surrounding its study; and the significance that it holds - for Muslims and for non-Muslims alike. Opening with a lucid overview of the rise and spread of Islam, from the seventh to twenty first century, the book charts the evolution of what was originally a small, localised community of believers into an international religion with over a billion adherents. Chapters are also dedicated to the peoples - Arabs, Persians, and Turks - who shaped Islamic history, and to three representative institutions - the mosque, jihad, and the caliphate - that highlight Islam's diversity over time.

'The book is extremely lucid, readable, sensibly organised, and wears its considerable learning, as they say, 'lightly'.'

BBC History Magazine

www.oup.com/vsi

GLOBALIZATION
A Very Short Introduction
Manfred Steger

'Globalization' has become one of the defining buzzwords of our time - a term that describes a variety of accelerating economic, political, cultural, ideological, and environmental processes that are rapidly altering our experience of the world. It is by its nature a dynamic topic - and this *Very Short Introduction* has been fully updated for 2009, to include developments in global politics, the impact of terrorism, and environmental issues. Presenting globalization in accessible language as a multifaceted process encompassing global, regional, and local aspects of social life, Manfred B. Steger looks at its causes and effects, examines whether it is a new phenomenon, and explores the question of whether, ultimately, globalization is a good or a bad thing.

www.oup.com/vsi

MODERN CHINA
A Very Short Introduction
Rana Mitter

China today is never out of the news: from human rights
controversies and the continued legacy of Tiananmen Square,
to global coverage of the Beijing Olympics, and the Chinese
'economic miracle'. It seems a country of contradictions: a
peasant society with some of the world's most futuristic cities,
heir to an ancient civilization that is still trying to find a modern
identity. This *Very Short Introduction* offers the reader with no
previous knowledge of China a variety of ways to understand
the world's most populous nation, giving a short, integrated
picture of modern Chinese society, culture, economy, politics
and art.

'A brilliant essay.'

Timothy Garton, TLS

INTERNATIONAL MIGRATION
A Very Short Introduction
Khalid Koser

Why has international migration become an issue of such intense public and political concern? How closely linked are migrants with terrorist organizations? What factors lie behind the dramatic increase in the number of women migrating? This *Very Short Introduction* examines the phenomenon of international human migration - both legal and illegal. Taking a global look at politics, economics, and globalization, the author presents the human side of topics such as asylum and refugees, human trafficking, migrant smuggling, development, and the international labour force.

www.oup.com/vsi